Science Concepts SECOND SERIES

Cells Revised Edition

Alvin Silverstein, Virginia Silverstein, and Laura Silverstein Nunn

 Twenty-First Century Books
Minneapolis

Twenty-First Century Books
A division of Lerner Publishing Group, Inc.
241 First Avenue North
Minneapolis, Minnesota 55401 U.S.A.

Website address: www.lernerbooks.com

Library of Congress Cataloging-in-Publication Data

Silverstein, Alvin.
    Cells. — Rev. ed. / by Alvin & Virginia Silverstein & Laura Silverstein Nunn.
        p.   cm. — (Science concepts, second series)
    Includes bibliographical references and index.
    ISBN 978–0–7613–3934–2 (lib. bdg. : alk. paper)
    1. Cells—Juvenile literature. 2. Cytology—Juvenile literature. I. Silverstein,
Virginia B. II. Nunn, Laura Silverstein. III. Title.
QH582.5.S538 2009
571.6—dc22   2007051038

Manufactured in the United States of America
1 2 3 4 5 6 – DP – 14 13 12 11 10 09

Contents

What do a fly, a mouse, and an elephant have in common? What about a goldfish, a lobster, and a whale? And what do they all have in common with a maple tree, a rosebush, and seaweed? All these things seem so different; what could they possibly have in common? For one thing, they are all alive. They have something else in common, too. Every living thing on Earth—including you—is made up of tiny units, called cells.

Building Blocks of Life

Cells are the "building blocks" of life. Most cells are so small you need a microscope to see them. Some living things have only one cell. These single-celled organisms are capable of living on their own and can do everything needed to support themselves. They live in ponds, rivers, lakes, and oceans. They can make or catch their own food and get rid of their wastes. They can respond and adapt to the environment. They can grow and reproduce—make new cells just like themselves. All these activities are

Above: *Like all animals and plants, those in this photo are made up of cells.*
Below: *These freshwater organisms are found in a drop of pond water.*

characteristic of living beings.

Most living creatures are multicellular organisms. They are made up of huge numbers of cells. Multicellular organisms include a wide variety of creatures—from tiny mosquitoes to snakes and elephants, grass and trees. The larger the organism, the more cells it contains.

How Many Cells?

Your body is made up of *trillions* of cells. (Scientists' estimates range from 10 trillion to 100 trillion.) Among Earth's organisms, you are just medium-size. A male African elephant (the largest land animal on Earth) weighs about 16,500 pounds (7,400 kilograms). That's about as much as 100 adult men. So a typical African elephant has more than 100 times as many body cells as you do—as many as a quadrillion!

Elephants have many more cells in their bodies than humans do.

A cell is like a tiny factory. Most cells have a control center that tells them what to do and when. Each cell has special structures that generate power for running all the cell's activities. The energy, in turn, powers the cell so it can eat or make food, grow, and reproduce. Other structures make complex chemicals to be used as building materials. Still others are involved in the many chemical reactions that go on constantly.

The cells of multicellular organisms are specialized for particular kinds of jobs. For instance, some cells carry messages from the brain to various parts of the body. Others help muscles make certain body parts move. There are also cells that keep making new blood, and still others work hard defending the body against injury and illness. All these cells work together to keep the organism alive and healthy.

Robert Hooke (1635–1703) named the tiny empty spaces in cork "cells." This name was later used for the basic unit of life.

The Discovery of Cells

In the seventeenth century, English scientist Robert Hooke coined the term "cell." In a book published in 1665, Hooke described his findings when he examined a slice of cork under a simple

microscope. He noticed that the cork appeared to be made up of a network of "little boxes." They reminded Hooke of the small cells, or rooms, of a monastery. So he called the empty little spaces "cells." He did not realize, however, that they had anything to do with living things.

In 1674, a Dutch lensmaker, Antoni van Leeuwenhoek, created a better microscope that allowed him to see very tiny objects up close. He observed what he called "animalcules" (little animals) swimming around in samples of pond water and even in scrapings from his own teeth. No one had seen this before. These tiny creatures were actually bacteria and protozoa, one-celled organisms. Again, there was no link made between this discovery and the concept that cells are the basic units of life.

Over time, the quality of microscopes improved. Many individual observations of cells were made in the eighteenth century. Then in the late 1830s, two German biologists, Matthias Schleiden

Antoni van Leeuwenhoek (1632–1723) created a microscope that allowed him to see single-celled organisms.

(a botanist) and Theodor Schwann (a zoologist) came up with a landmark theory about cells. They suggested that all living things are made up of cells and that cells are the basic units of life. These ideas became known as the cell theory.

In 1858, the cell theory was expanded by a German pathologist, Rudolf Virchow. He stated that all cells come from previously existing cells. This seemed to imply that life is an unbroken chain stretching back to the beginning of life on Earth. According to Virchow's theory, generations of cells have continued through billions of years of evolution, from the first primitive cells to the complex and varied organisms of today.

Rudolph Virchow (1821–1921) said that all cells are formed from cells that already existed—all the way back to the first living cells on Earth. Virchow was the first to expand cell theory into evolution.

chapter two

Cells: The Inside Story

Under a powerful microscope, scientists can get an amazing close-up view of a single tiny living cell. They have found that cells come in many different shapes and sizes. Some cells look like tiny ice cubes; others are long and thin. There are cells that look like little rods, balls, or doughnuts without the hole in the middle. Others look like kites or tadpoles. Some have no fixed shape at all, but simply look like blobs of jelly. Scientists who study cells have found that a single cell may be as large as a tennis ball or so small that thousands of them would fit on the period at the end of this sentence.

As microscopes became more powerful, scientists could see inside the cells and found that there are two main kinds. One, called the prokaryote, is a relatively simple form. This type includes single-celled bacteria, such as the germs that cause strep throat, tuberculosis, and other illnesses. Other cells are more complex. Their contents are organized into distinct structures that are specialized for specific functions. These cells are found in eukaryotes, which range from tiny, single-celled pond creatures to plants and animals, whose bodies may contain trillions of cells.

The Simplest Cells

Prokaryotes are among the simplest and smallest of all living things. All living things, even the most primitive cells, contain material called DNA (deoxyribonucleic acid). This substance contains genes, units of heredity. Genes carry the instructions that determine the characteristics of a cell and

A chicken egg (left) *and an ostrich egg* (right) *each consist of a single cell.*

blueprints for making new cells. In more organized cells—those of eukaryotes—DNA is stored in a structure called a nucleus, which is surrounded by a nuclear membrane, keeping it separate from the rest of the cell's contents.

DNA Double Helix

Strands:

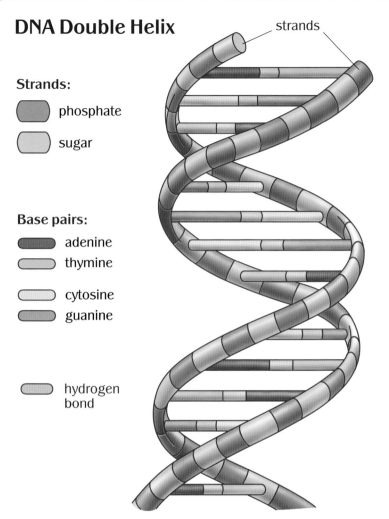

phosphate

sugar

Base pairs:

adenine
thymine

cytosine
guanine

hydrogen
bond

*This model shows the chemical structure of a small portion
of DNA. Two long threadlike strands containing sugar and
phosphate form the backbone. Chemicals called nitrogen
bases stick out and can bond together, joining the two
strands. DNA contains four kinds of bases. Like letters of
the alphabet, these bases spell out the words, sentences, and
chapters in the cell's genetic "instruction book." DNA is
twisted into a spiral staircase shape called a double helix.*

Prokaryotes, on the other hand, do not have a distinct nucleus. (The term "prokaryote" means "before nucleus"; "eukaryote" means "true nucleus.") Although prokaryotes do not have a real nucleus, they do have a nuclear area, called a nucleoid, that contains DNA. The DNA is not surrounded by a membrane and is, therefore, exposed to the rest of the cell's contents.

What does a simple cell look like? Let's take a look at a bacterium. A bacterial cell is wrapped in a stretchy, baglike covering called the plasma membrane. The plasma membrane contains tiny pores or openings that allow small molecules to pass into the cell. Around the plasma membrane is a cell wall. This is a tough layer that protects the bacterium. Some bacteria also have another protective layer called a capsule. This slimy layer, wrapped around the cell wall, protects the bacterium from harmful chemicals and keeps it from drying out.

In many species, long hairlike structures called flagella extend through the layers and help the bacterium move. These flagella are very different from those of other single-celled organisms. A bacterium's flagellum is just a single fiber; the flagella of other living things are much more complicated.

Long flagella are seen extending outside this bacterium, E. coli. Instead of whipping back and forth as other flagella do, a bacterium's corkscrew-shaped flagella rotate at the place where they are connected to the cell. In this way, they work like a ship's propeller to push the bacterium along.

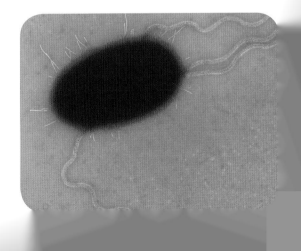

Inside the cell is a jellylike substance called cytoplasm. The cytoplasm contains long threadlike structures called chromosomes. Chromosomes carry DNA, the bacterium's genetic instructions for running all the cell's activities. Most bacteria have only a single chromosome. The ends of the long DNA are joined, forming a ring. Some bacteria have a bit of extra DNA in the form of small rings called plasmids.

The cytoplasm is also full of tiny spherical structures called ribosomes, which are involved in making proteins, complex chemicals that do various jobs for the cell. One of the chemicals that helps to form the ribosomes is RNA (ribonucleic acid). RNA has a somewhat similar chemical structure to DNA. Several different kinds of RNA are involved in making proteins. The cytoplasm also contains many kinds of enzymes: special chemicals that help build different parts of the cell or break down food.

The "Typical" Cell

Most living things, including single-cell protists, fungi, plants, and animals, are made up of eukaryotic cells. Eukaryotes are not really more complicated than prokaryotes; rather, they are much more organized. You can think of a eukaryotic cell as a house. A house has many rooms, and each one has a special function. For instance, there may be a kitchen, a living room, and a bedroom. A eukaryotic cell has many "rooms," called organelles (little organs). Like the rooms of a house, each organelle has a different function.

Animal Cell

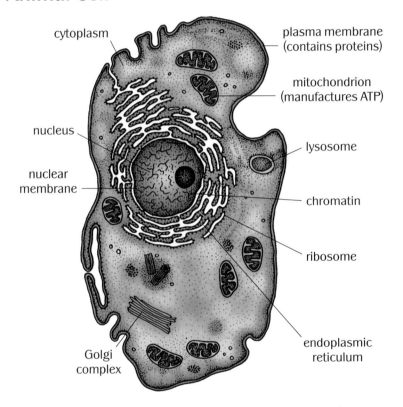

An animal cell contains a number of specialized structures (called organelles), which do various jobs for the cell. Different kinds of animal cells have characteristic shapes that may differ greatly from this "typical" animal cell.

Let's take a look at a typical animal cell. The largest organelle is the nucleus. This is the cell's control center. It houses chromosomes, which contain DNA. Remember, DNA contains the genetically coded instructions for the cell's activities, including cell growth and reproduction. Parts of the DNA are continually turned on and off as the nucleus receives chemical messages from the rest of the cell and the world outside. The "turned on" parts are copied into pieces of RNA that move out through pores in the nuclear membrane into the cytoplasm. This kind of RNA is called messenger RNA because it carries messages from the control

Can't Live without It . . .

Just how important is the nucleus to a living cell? Scientists have done a number of experiments to find out. In one experiment, a researcher, using a microscope and working with very tiny tools, surgically removed the nucleus from a single-celled amoeba (a pond-dweller that looks like a blob of jelly). Afterward, the amoeba was unable to eat and grow. It died a few weeks later. However, if the amoeba was given a new nucleus after a day or two, it made a complete recovery. So a nucleus is actually essential to a cell's life.

center out to the rest of the cell. Messenger RNA provides the blueprints for making proteins.

The nucleus also contains small rounded structures called nucleoli. Protein molecules move into the nucleoli and combine with a kind of RNA called ribosomal RNA. This forms parts of ribosomes, which move out of the nucleus and into the cytoplasm. There they are put together to form working ribosomes.

A thin plasma membrane, which is made of two layers of a fatty substance, surrounds the entire cell. The nucleus and the other organelles are also wrapped in their own membranes. The membranes hold all the parts of the cell together, yet keep them separate at the same time. Tiny pores allow only

. . . or Can They?

Our bodies have one kind of cell that doesn't have a nucleus. Each red blood cell starts out with a nucleus, but by the time it matures and enters the bloodstream, its nucleus has disappeared. It is still "alive" and continues to work for the body, carrying materials for the cells and taking away their waste products, but it is doomed. As it squeezes through the narrow blood vessels, it may become damaged, but it cannot repair itself the way other cells do. It also cannot reproduce to make more blood cells. Gradually, damages build up, until the red cell finally breaks open and spills out its contents. Most red blood cells die just a few months after they have entered the blood.

You Know?

ryotic cells have
where from 2
ore than 1,000
mosomes. Each
ains a molecule
NA, attached to
eins. The single
nosome found in
prokaryotic cells
tains only DNA.

necessary materials to pass through the membrane and screen out those that are unacceptable or harmful. Proteins, embedded in the fatty membrane like the raisins in a slice of raisin bread, also help to transport substances into and out of the cell and its organelles.

Many of the cell's activities take place in the cytoplasm. Researchers used to think that the cytoplasm was just a jellylike material in which the organelles floated. When high-power electron microscopes were developed, however, scientists discovered that eukaryotic cells have a highly organized structure. Branching off from the nucleus is a network of tubelike membranes called endoplasmic reticulum (ER). The ER runs through the cytoplasm and joins with the plasma membrane at the outside of the cell. Some of the ER membranes have smooth surfaces and are known as smooth ER; others are covered with active ribosomes and are called rough ER. Proteins are produced here.

A stack of six to twenty saucer-shaped membrane bags makes up the Golgi complex. This organelle is like a sorting and packaging factory. As proteins move up the stack, they go through chemical changes to produce the special substances that cells need.

Plasma Membrane

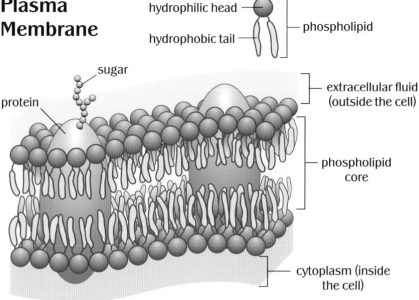

hydrophilic head
hydrophobic tail
phospholipid

sugar
protein

extracellular fluid (outside the cell)

phospholipid core

cytoplasm (inside the cell)

The plasma membrane is a double layer, made mostly of fatty substances called phospholipids. Proteins are embedded in the lipid layers, and there are some sugars on the surface. Phospholipids are chemicals made of two very different parts: the phospho part is hydrophilic (water-loving) and the lipid parts are hydrophobic (water-fearing). The two layers are arranged so that the hydrophilic parts are on the outer and inner surfaces of the membrane and the hydrophobic parts are in the middle. Only very small molecules, such as oxygen and carbon dioxide, and oily substances can move directly through the membrane. Other materials are transported through the membrane by proteins.

Some are used inside the cell itself; others pass out through the plasma membrane and are sent to other cells in the organism. The ER and Golgi bodies both help in transporting materials within the cells.

Small round organelles called lysosomes are the cell's trash bins. They are filled with powerful enzymes that are ready to digest various kinds of cell chemicals, from DNA and RNA to proteins, fats, and carbohydrates (sugars and starches). When organelles get worn out, they are sent to the lysosomes to be broken down and recycled. Foreign particles, including invading germs, are also digested in the lysosomes. Sometimes, however, lysosomes can cause trouble. Their enzymes may leak out and start digesting the cell contents, and the cell may die.

Cells need energy to power their activities. All the cell's energy is generated in football-shaped structures called mitochondria. Each cell may contain hundreds of mitochondria. The energy is stored in a chemical compound called ATP (adenosine triphosphate). ATP provides a ready source of energy for a variety of chemical reactions. Animals also use ATP to store small amounts of energy for short periods of time. Any extra energy is stored in more complex chemicals, starches, and fats.

Special Delivery

Until the 1980s, scientists thought that proteins and various other biochemicals just floated through the cytoplasm until they reached their destination. But powerful electron microscopes revealed that the cytoplasm is crisscrossed by huge numbers of thin, threadlike tubes linked together like a microscopic Tinkertoy. These are like a 3-D subway system on which membrane-wrapped chemical packages are transported from one part of the cell to another.

Each package carries an address label: a chemical on its surface with a particular shape that fits exactly into a docking site (called a receptor) on the membrane of the organelle to which it is being sent. Receptors are very specific. Like a lock that only one key can fit, they will accept only one particular kind of chemical package. When the right substance arrives, it binds to the receptor and then is allowed into the organelle.

Plant Cells Are Different

The "typical cell" we have been describing is an animal cell. Plant cells have some additional

Plant Cell

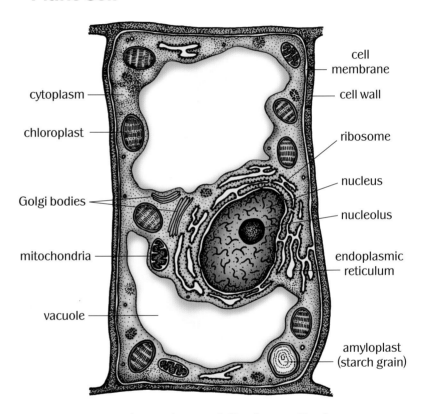

A plant cell contains various specialized organelles. Some are similar to those in animal cells. Others, such as chloroplasts and vacuoles, are found only in plants. Plant cells are wrapped in a tough cell wall, which gives them a firmer, more squared-off shape than animal cells.

structures that are not found in animal cells. Plant cells are wrapped in a thick, rigid outer cell wall that is different from a bacterial cell wall. This kind of cell wall is made mostly of a tough material called cellulose. Cellulose makes plant stems stiff.

Take a Bite Out of Cellulose

Cellulose is too tough for our bodies to digest. Yet some organisms, including bacteria and some insects, can digest cellulose.

Cows and rabbits live on grass and other plant leaves, but they can't digest cellulose on their own. A cow has a four-part stomach. In the first part, a pouch called the rumen, millions of bacteria produce chemicals that break down the tough cellulose in the grass that the cow swallows. After a few hours, the cow "burps up" a mouthful of the partly digested material (called the cud) and chews and swallows it again. Then the cud passes through the second, third, and fourth stomach chambers to complete the digestion process. Rabbits also play host to helpful bacteria that digest the cellulose in the plants they eat. These bacteria live in a special pouch in the rabbits' intestines, called the caecum.

Plant cells collect the energy of sunlight in organelles called chloroplasts. Chloroplasts contain chlorophyll, a green pigment that absorbs the sun's rays. This is the first step in photosynthesis, a

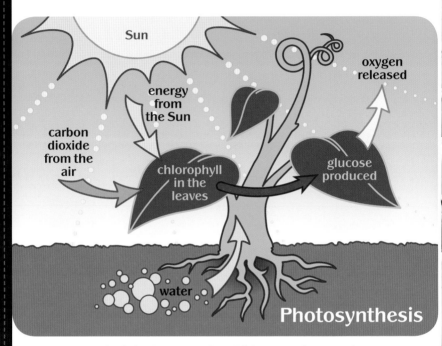

Sun

energy from the Sun

oxygen released

carbon dioxide from the air

chlorophyll in the leaves

glucose produced

water

Photosynthesis

Photosynthesis is the process by which green plants make their food. The process begins when sunlight interacts with the chlorophyll in the plant's leaves and light energy is stored as chemical energy in the chloroplasts. Water and carbon dioxide also enter the leaf. The carbon dioxide combines with water, using the energy stored in the chloroplasts, to produce sugar. The sugar is then transported to other parts of the plant and either stored, used right away for energy, or used to make other food substances.

process that allows plants to make their own food. The sunlight energy powers a series of chemical reactions in which carbon dioxide from the air and water from the soil are turned into sugar. The sugar can then be converted to more complex chemicals, such as starch, which is used to store food. The cellulose that forms the plant's cell wall is also made from sugar. In other reactions, the plant cell can combine sugar with raw materials from the soil to form proteins, fats, and other complex chemicals the plant needs. Like animal cells, plant cells also have mitochondria, which are used to release energy from stored foods.

Chloroplasts belong to a larger group of organelles called plastids. Plants typically have two other kinds of plastids in addition to their chloroplasts. Chromoplasts are plastids that

This image of green algae shows the chloroplasts, which are dark green patches within the cells.

Some of these vegetables, including the tomatoes, changed color when the chloroplasts turned into chromoplasts.

contain different colored pigments, usually yellow, orange, or red ("chromo" means color). Sometimes chloroplasts turn into chromoplasts. This is what happens when a fruit, such as an apple or tomato, ripens. First it is green, but then it gradually turns to bright red as the chromoplasts in the plant cells produce red pigments. The third main type of plastids, leucoplasts, do not contain any pigments, so they are not colored ("leuco" means white). They are used for storing food, such as starches. Sometimes, when they are exposed to light, leucoplasts may turn into chloroplasts. That is what happens when a white potato, kept in the light, turns green.

If you looked at a plant cell under a microscope, it would appear mostly hollow. This isn't just an empty space; it is a baglike structure called a vacuole. Vacuoles are strapped to the cell by a membrane. This membranous bag actually makes up about 90 percent of each plant cell. Vacuoles aren't as hollow as they appear. They are filled with a liquid called cell sap, which contains water, salts, and sugars. The liquid-filled vacuoles help to keep plant leaves and stems from getting limp. The cell sap may also contain dissolved proteins and brightly colored pigments. These pigments produce the red and blue colors of many vegetables and fruits, such as radishes, turnips, grapes, plums, blueberries, and cherries. Red and blue flowers, such as roses, geraniums, and cornflowers, get their color from pigments in their vacuoles. The vacuoles in plant cells are also used for temporary storing of materials or getting rid of excess water and waste products from the cell. They provide safe storage for chemicals that could kill the cell if they remained in the cytoplasm.

You started your life as a single cell. That cell divided and divided again and then became a ball of cells. As it got bigger, parts of it started to change. Soon there was a distinct head, body, and a little tail. Eventually, buds on the sides grew into arms and legs. Meanwhile, the body grew and the tail disappeared. Eyes, ears, nose, and mouth formed on the head. Inside the body, internal organs developed: a beating heart, lungs that weren't functioning yet, a stomach, and all the other structures that make up a human being.

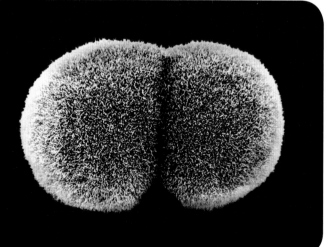

This mammal egg is dividing into two.

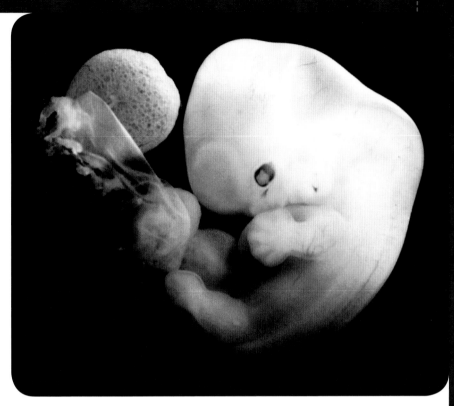

The cells of a human embryo continue to divide and increase in number as the embryo grows and develops.

For nine months you grew and developed inside your mother's body. After you were born, you continued to grow. You will go on growing and developing through your teen years. Through all this growth, from the first cell to a baby, a child, and finally an adult, the number of cells in the body increases. This happens by cell division, a process in

Did You Know?

Cell division continues throughout your entire life. Biologists estimate that more than 25 million cells go through cell division every second of your life.

which a single cell grows and splits into two cells. Even after growth has stopped, cell division is still important. When cells get injured or wear out, they need to be replaced. That is how you can heal a cut on your finger or even a broken bone in your leg. All these cell divisions that we have described are of a particular kind, called mitosis.

How One Cell Becomes Two

Before cell division begins, a cell must make a copy of its genetic instructions. A cell that divides is called a mother cell; its offspring are known as daughter cells. When a cell divides by mitosis, the two daughter cells that form are smaller copies of the original cell. Each daughter cell gets a complete copy of all the DNA instructions its parent had. The daughter cells can then become mother cells to their own daughter cells, passing along the same genes they inherited from their mother, and the process continues.

When a prokaryote reproduces, it simply splits into two. Once the cell gets to a certain size, it makes a copy of all its DNA. Then it grows a new piece of plasma membrane down the middle of the cell, separating the old and new sets of DNA. After that, the cell divides into two daughter cells. With a complete set of genes and just the right building blocks, the two daughter cells can grow, and the cycle starts all over again. This process is known as binary fission (which means "splitting into two").

Cell division in eukaryotes is much more complex than binary fission. In animals, the process actually starts long before signs of it can be seen through a microscope. During this time, called the interphase, the cell grows and then gets ready to divide. It makes an exact copy of all its DNA, which at this time is in the form of long, thin threads. They are spread out in a tangled network called chromatin. Now the cell is ready to start vthe actual division.

Mitosis involves four distinct stages: prophase, metaphase, anaphase, and telophase. As the cell passes through these separate stages, the chromatin strands get thicker and shorter, forming pairs of rod-shaped chromosomes.

These chromosomes first line up across the middle of the cell and then move apart so that one of each pair ends up at the opposite "poles" of the cell. The cell, which now has two distinct nuclei, pinches in at the middle and splits into two cells. (Scientists call the division of the cytoplasm cytokinesis.) Because all of the DNA was copied before mitosis began, each daughter cell has one full set of chromosomes.

Stages of Mitosis

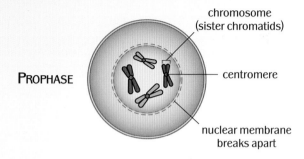

chromosome
(sister chromatids)

PROPHASE

centromere

nuclear membrane
breaks apart

Prophase: The chromosomes become short and thick and coil together into two thick rods ("sister chromatids"), joined together at the centromere. The DNA has already been copied, so each chromatid is a duplicate of the other. Thus, each sister chromatid contains the same genetic information. Before the cell can divide, these sister chromatids must separate from one another. The nuclear membrane starts to break down. Meanwhile, in the cytoplasm, two tiny organelles (centrioles) divide, and the pairs begin to move apart. As they separate, they pull out a group of thin fibers attached to the chromatids, forming a football-shaped network, the spindle. The spindle fibers pull on the chromatids, which then begin to move toward the middle of the cell.

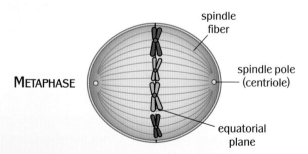

spindle
fiber

METAPHASE

spindle pole
(centriole)

equatorial
plane

Metaphase: The chromatids, still attached together in pairs, line up with their centromeres along a plane through the middle of the cell. This plane (the equatorial plane) cuts through the middle of the spindle, midway between the two centrioles. It is like the Earth's equator, and the centrioles are like the North and South poles.

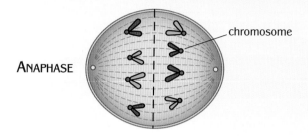

ANAPHASE

chromosome

Anaphase: The centromeres that held the sister chromatids together divide. Now the sister chromatids have become separate chromosomes. They begin to move apart, toward the opposite poles of ther spindle. One of each pair moves toward one pole, while the other sister chromatid moves toward the opposite pole.

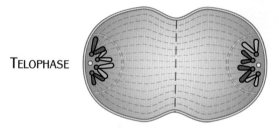

TELOPHASE

Telophase: The chromosomes have reached the opposite poles. Now it is like watching a movie of the prophase run backward. The spindle disappears, the nuclear membrane re-forms, and the chromosomes stretch out into thin strands of chromatin.

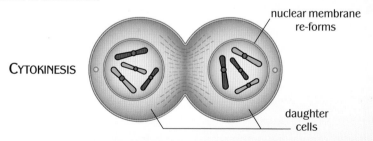

nuclear membrane
re-forms

CYTOKINESIS

daughter
cells

Cytokinesis: Division of the cytoplasm follows the division of the nucleus. Contracting fibers pinch in around the middle of the cell between the two nuclei. The pinching continues, much like the way pulling a drawstring narrows the waist of a pair of sweatpants. Finally the "waist" is tightened so much that the cytoplasm is separated into two new daughter cells.

Cell division in plants is similar to that in animals, with a few main differences. Plant cells do not have centrioles, although a spindle forms just as it does in animal cells. A plant cell cannot complete its division by pinching in at its "waist" because it is surrounded by a stiff cell wall. During cytokinesis, the Golgi complex produces membrane-covered "bags" of carbohydrates that line up along the equator between the two nuclei. These bags come together to form a structure called the cell plate. Eventually, the cell plate forms a new cell wall that completely separates the two daughter cells. The membrane covers of the bags form part of the cell membranes of the daughter cells.

What Is Mitosis Good For?

All living things are brought into the world by processes involving mitosis. A single-celled organism may reproduce simply by dividing in two. A multicellular organism begins life as a single cell, which must divide many times before becoming a recognizable member of the species.

Mitosis is necessary for all growth, whether it be for a tree growing longer branches or a child growing another inch taller. As an organism grows, mitosis is responsible for building and developing until the organism reaches its full potential. But mitosis doesn't stop there. Cells that get damaged, diseased, or worn out have to be replaced. Every second, millions of cells in your body die. If you couldn't replace these lost cells, you would die in a matter of days. The dead cells are replaced through mitosis, so a multicellular organism can go on living.

Your body has many different kinds of cells, but only certain cells are constantly being produced. For instance, every time you touch something, you shed dead skin cells. New skin cells are constantly forming, and they live only about twenty-eight days. The new cells push the older ones toward the surface. The older cells are squeezed together and flattened, and finally they die. They contain a protein that forms a thick, outer coat that helps to protect the soft, living cells underneath.

Blood cells also have a relatively short life span. Red blood cells live for only 120 days. In order to keep a good blood

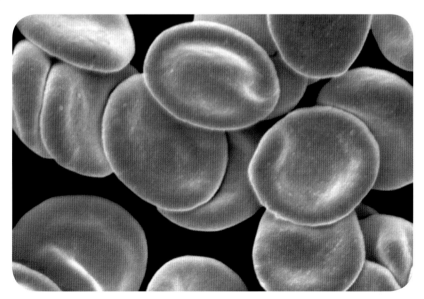

Red blood cells are just one kind of cell in your body that are constantly being reproduced.

supply, the blood-forming cells in the marrow in your bones make 100 million new red cells every minute! Lining cells, such as those inside your mouth, are also constantly forming new ones.

Some cells, such as the nerve cells and muscle cells, do not usually divide after early childhood. When you exercise, for example, your muscles may get bigger, but you are not growing extra muscle cells. Instead, the muscle cells you already have are getting larger.

Cells Gone Wild

New cells are constantly forming to replace those that die. Normally, cells reproduce at just the right rate to replace the dying cells. Cell division is generally controlled through chemical signals given off by certain cells to other cells in the body. Contact with the cells around it may also tell a body cell to divide or not to divide.

Cancer cells do not act this way. Although they don't divide any faster than normal cells, cancer cells cannot control their reproduction. Then cell division gets out of control. This happens because at some point, the cancer cells change or mutate. They lose the ability to pick up and respond to signals that

This cancer cell (center) can be seen among healthy epithelial cells in a human lung.

control cell division. So they keep dividing and can't stop. They crawl over other cells and push their way into healthy tissues. Cancer cells have also lost some of their specialized functions and do not work for the good of the body. Soon they start to choke out normal, healthy, functioning cells that have important jobs to do, such as making blood, digesting food, or controlling the movements of body parts. The cancer cells also steal food and other materials the body cells need to live.

Cancer cells can cause so much damage to the body cells that they may even kill the organism. Cancer can affect people at any age, most species of animals, and even many kinds of plants.

Even nerve and muscle cells in adults' bodies have some ability to repair damage. If a nerve cell's genetic material is still intact, for example, it can grow new branches and make new connections with nerve and muscle cells. Until recently, however, scientists believed that an adult's body cannot form new nerve or muscle cells to replace cells that have died. In the late 1990s and early 2000s, studies began to show that this old view was wrong. Heart muscle damaged by a heart attack

The tail of this salamander is beginning to grow back. This is an example of regeneration, which occurs by mitosis.

can grow new heart muscle cells. The brain does continue
to produce new neurons (nerve cells) throughout life. And
these new neurons quickly take part in the formation of new
memories. Researchers are searching for ways to stimulate
mitosis in nerve and muscle cells, to develop better treatments
for paralysis and heart disease.

chapter four

Making a New Life

What would our world be like if people reproduced by mitosis? Many of Earth's organisms do just that. Bacteria, for example, usually reproduce by simply splitting in half. So do single-celled pond organisms, such as amoebas and paramecia. The cell makes a copy of its DNA and then divides into two smaller copies of itself. These daughter cells are identical "twins." Each has a complete set of its parent's hereditary instructions. If people reproduced this way, we would all be alike. Except for a few small differences caused by errors in copying a cell's DNA, there would be no variation.

Actually, though, if reproduction took place only by mitosis, there wouldn't be any people. We would all be single-celled creatures living in ponds or oceans. Evolution—the gradual development of new kinds of organisms by changes in their genes—could not

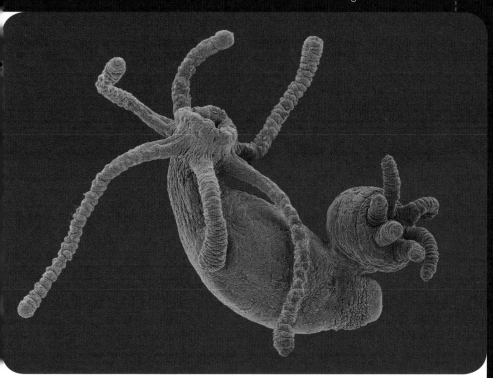

A small hydra is budding asexually from its parent.

have occurred. However, some multicellular organisms do use mitosis to produce a new generation.

Both single-celled and multicellular organisms can reproduce by a type of mitosis called budding. In yeasts (which are single-celled eukaryotes), the parent cell produces a bud, a small knob containing a copy of the parent's DNA. The bud bulges out from the parent cell, grows a bit, then separates while it is still much smaller. Tiny multicellular pond creatures called hydras form buds in much the same way as the single-celled yeasts. A hydra has a vase-shaped body, topped by a crown of tentacles. The bud that forms on an adult hydra is a miniature copy of its parent. When it has grown large enough to survive on its own, the bud breaks off and swims away.

Mitosis in the Garden

If you put the branches trimmed from a hedge in water, roots will grow out of the bottom of the cut stems. Planted in soil, these rooted cuttings will grow into new bushes. These new plants are formed by simple cell division—mitosis.

Other plants can also reproduce by mitosis. Strawberry plants send out runners, long stems that snake out along the ground and then send down roots. Soon leaves and flowers form, too. If the runner is cut, the new strawberry plant can live on its own. Grasses and ivy can form new plants in a similar way. Plants like tulips and daffodils, which grow from bulbs, can also reproduce by mitosis. During the growing season, the plant forms more bulbs down in the soil. The following spring, each bulb forms a new plant.

These strawberry plants started out as a single mother plant. It sent out new shoots (runners), which will send roots into the ground at different places and form complete, new plants there.

Scientists refer to the forms of reproduction by mitosis as asexual reproduction. A single parent forms daughters that are just like it.

Sexual Reproduction

At some point in the long evolution of life on Earth, living organisms came up with a new idea. Two organisms of the same single-celled species came together and exchanged some of their genetic material. Then, when they divided, their offspring were not exactly like either of them but, instead, shared some of the traits of each parent. This mix-and-match kind of reproduction had some important advantages. It produced much more varied organisms that were better able to adapt to changes in the environment. This was the start of sexual reproduction. Even some bacteria today can take part in a kind of "mating" that shuffles their genes. So can single-celled eukaryotes.

As life evolved further, sexual reproduction became more complex. Specialized organs developed to produce reproductive cells. These cells had only one function: to join with those of another organism of the same species to produce offspring. The "sex cells" had to be of a new, special type, because mitosis would not work very well in sexual reproduction. Think about it. Let's say a particular kind of animal has twenty chromosomes in each of its cells. If its sex cells had twenty chromosomes, then when they joined with those of another animal, they would produce offspring with forty chromosomes in each cell. The next generation would have eighty chromosomes in each cell. It would not be long before there were far too many chromosomes to fit into a cell. So sexual reproduction must include some way to keep the number of chromosomes the same in the next generation. This occurs by way of a special kind of cell division, called meiosis.

How Meiosis Works

When a cell divides in meiosis, each new cell formed receives only half of the original set of DNA. The new cells are not normal body cells; they are sex cells. They are produced only in the reproductive organs. The sex cells of a female are called eggs, or ova. Those of a male are called sperm. They are the key to sexual reproduction: a sex cell from a male joins with a sex cell from a female to form a single, combined cell, the zygote. This process is called fertilization, and the cell that results can develop into a whole new individual. The zygote has a full set of DNA because it received a half set from each parent. So the new organism is not exactly like its mother or just like its father. Rather it has a mixture of both of its parents' genes. As a result, a new, unique individual is born.

The purpose of meiosis is to produce the sex cells needed for reproduction. Before meiosis, these

You Know?
are sometimes
spermatozoa.
zoa part means
ls." Sperm look
tadpoles and
around actively
little animals.

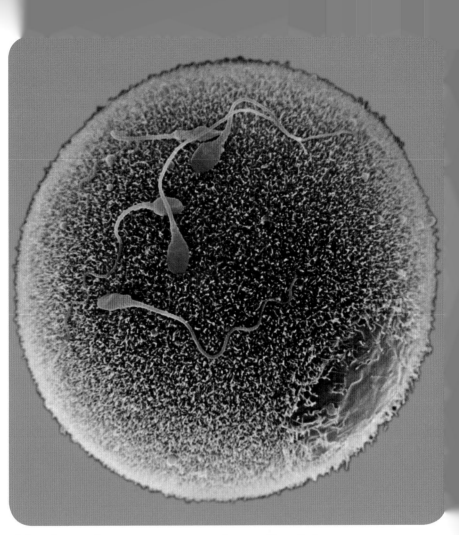

A female sex cell, or ovum, attracts male sex cells, called sperm.

cells are known as germ cells. They have nothing to do with disease-causing germs. Germ cells are cells that have the potential to develop into sex cells.

In a young individual, all cells are diploid—they have two of each kind of chromosome. Two chromosomes of the same kind are referred to as a homologous pair. Each homologous pair includes one chromosome from

These nursing kittens are the result of the combined genetic material of their parents.

the organism's mother and one from its father. Homologous chromosomes look similar, but they do not contain the same genetic material. When a diploid germ cell undergoes meiosis, each homologous pair is divided between the two daughter cells. The new cells are haploid cells, each with half as many chromosomes as its mother cell. Each haploid cell contains only one of each type of chromosome. (The term haploid does not mean half a set of chromosomes. In fact, haploid cells have a full, single set.)

Meiosis is similar to mitosis in some ways, but there are some important differences. In mitosis, there is a single cell division, which divides a cell into two daughter cells. Meiosis, on the other hand, involves two processes of cell division, ultimately producing four daughter cells. These two divisions are known as meiosis I and meiosis II. The stages in both mitosis and meiosis have the same names, but meiosis involves some very different processes.

Meiosis in Animals

Let's take a look at meiosis in animals. Like mitosis, meiosis starts in the interphase, before the actual cell division begins. During this time, the diploid cell makes copies of all its DNA. So as meiosis I begins, each chromosome consists of two sister chromatids, joined at their centromeres. In the first division of meiosis, the sister chromatids stay joined, but the homologous pairs of chromosomes are divided between the two daughter cells that are formed. Then a second division follows, without an interphase. The DNA of each daughter cell is not copied this time. So when the daughter cells divide, each new cell is left with only half of the original set of DNA—half the number of chromosomes.

Stages of Meiosis

Meiosis I

Prophase I: The chromosomes, which have already been copied, start to thicken and condense. Then each chromosome, which now consists of two joined sister chromatids, is drawn to the other chromosome in its homologous pair (which also has a sister chromatid). The homologous chromosomes—one from the mother (maternal) and one from the father (paternal)—line up alongside one another, much like zipping up the two sides of a jacket. The two homologous pairs join together to form a tetrad, a structure that includes four chromatids. The maternal and paternal chromosomes now cross over one another at points called chiasmata, where they may swap genetic material. This process, called crossing over, creates new combinations of genes that were not present in either parent. Meanwhile, the nucleolus and nuclear membrane break apart. Soon the spindle forms, and spindle poles become apparent.

Metaphase I: The homologous pairs get ready to separate. The tetrads (paired homologous chromatids) line up along the equator of the spindle in a plane called the metaphase plate. Both chromatids of one chromosome are turned toward the same pole. The sister chromatids of the homologous chromosome are turned toward the opposite pole.

Anaphase I: The spindle fibers attached to each chromosome shorten, pulling the homologous

Meiosis I

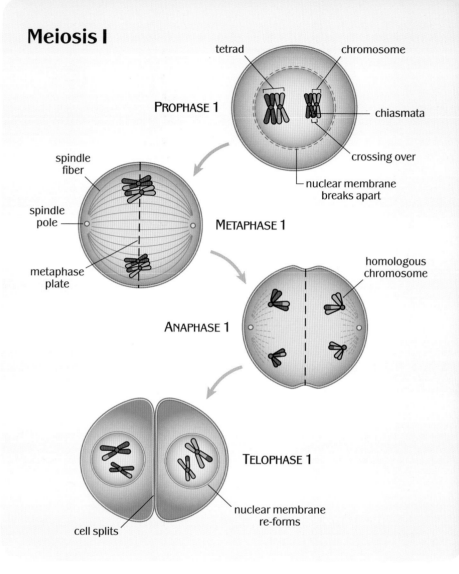

tetrad

chromosome

PROPHASE 1

chiasmata

crossing over

nuclear membrane breaks apart

spindle fiber

spindle pole

METAPHASE 1

metaphase plate

homologous chromosome

ANAPHASE 1

TELOPHASE 1

nuclear membrane re-forms

cell splits

chromosomes of each tetrad to opposite spindle poles. The sister chromatids of each chromosome are still linked at their centromeres, but the tetrad is finally separated.

Telophase I: The nuclear membranes re-form. Cytokinesis then takes place, splitting the diploid cell into two haploid cells.

Meiosis II

Prophase II: The chromosomes shorten and thicken. The spindle re-forms, and the sister chromatids move toward the cell's metaphase plate.

Metaphase II: The chromosomes line up along the equator. The sister chromatids of each chromosome are attached to the spindle fibers, which lead to opposite poles of the cell.

Anaphase II: The chromatids split, and the newly independent chromosomes are pulled toward opposite spindle poles.

Telophase II: A nuclear membrane forms around each group of chromosomes, producing nuclei. The cell divides through cytokinesis, forming two haploid daughter cells. Since the other cell from meiosis I goes through the same process, meiosis II produces a total of four haploid daughter cells from the original parent. Each daughter cell has half of the chromosomes of the original diploid cell (although each chromosome may contain different genetic information due to crossing over).

In males, the four cells that result from meiosis are sperm. Each one consists of a "head" (which contains the haploid chromosome set) and a "tail" (a long, whiplike flagellum) that allows the sperm to swim actively. Each sperm is only one-quarter the size of the original cell because the cytoplasm was divided evenly among them in the cell divisions of meiosis.

Meiosis II

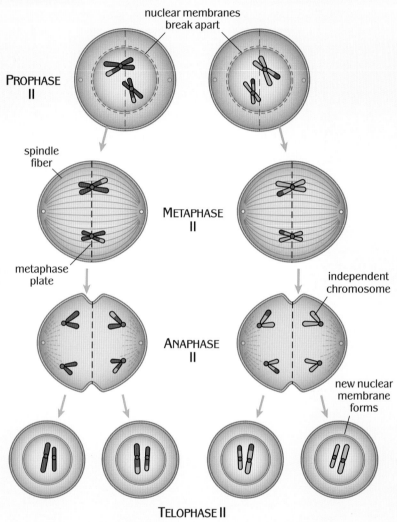

nuclear membranes break apart

PROPHASE II

spindle fiber

METAPHASE II

metaphase plate

independent chromosome

ANAPHASE II

new nuclear membrane forms

TELOPHASE II

In females, meiosis is more complicated. When the daughter cells separate at the end of meiosis I, one of them receives nearly all of the cytoplasm from the original cell.

In mitosis, prophase usually takes only a few minutes, but prophase I of meiosis can last for hours or even years. When a human female is born, for example, all of the sex cells that will eventually form ova have already entered prophase I. They stay in this phase until the girl matures. Then, each month, one of the cells starts into the next stage of meiosis.

So one daughter cell is much bigger than the other. The small daughter cell divides in meiosis II to produce two tiny cells called polar bodies. Each one is basically a nucleus wrapped in a membrane. Meanwhile, the big daughter cell goes through another uneven division at the end of meiosis II. The result is another polar body and a large egg cell (ovum). The ovum has received nearly all of the original cell's cytoplasm, along with one haploid set of chromosomes.

Why is meiosis so complicated in females? The egg cell must provide food for the early development of a new individual. If the divisions of meiosis produced equal-size cells, each would have only a one-quarter-size portion of food. The unequal divisions allow the ovum to end up with the largest possible amount of food. In case you're wondering what happens to the polar bodies—they break down and disappear. Each one contains a whole haploid set of chromosomes, but they are just "throwaways."

Meiosis in Plants

In plants, meiosis is basically similar to the process in animals, but it can produce either four gametes (male or female sex cells) or four spores. Spores are haploid cells that divide by mitosis to produce a whole individual, with only one haploid set of chromosomes. This kind of reproduction occurs in many algae and in plants such as ferns. These haploid organisms eventually produce gametes, which can join with a gamete of the opposite sex to form a zygote that develops into a diploid organism. There is thus an alternation of generations, with the plant or alga spending part of its life in a haploid phase and part of its life in a diploid phase.

The underside of this fern leaf shows spores.

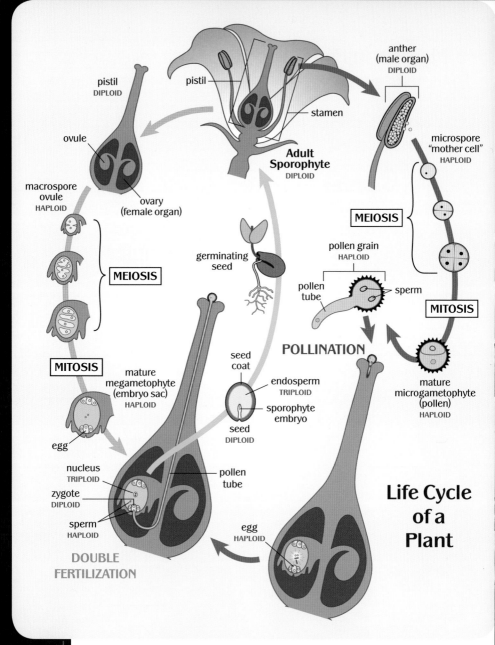

Life Cycle of a Plant

Meiosis in flowering plants is more complicated than in animals. It results in double fertilization, producing a diploid zygote and triploid endosperm.

In the flowering plants, spores exist in the reproductive organs: the anthers (male organs) and ovaries (female organs). Meiosis in the anthers produces pollen grains (which contain two sperm) and tube cells that will help the sperm get to the female sex cells. In the ovary, meiosis is even more complicated, producing a structure called the embryo sac. When sperm reach the ovary, a double fertilization occurs. One sperm from a pollen grain fertilizes an egg cell, producing a zygote that will grow into a new plant. The other sperm joins with a special cell that has two nuclei, producing a triploid cell—one with three sets of chromosomes. This new cell develops into endosperm, the portion of the seed containing stored food. The endosperm gives the new plant a head start in life. It supports the development of the embryo, its sprouting, and the early growth of the seedling until it is able to make its own food.

Specialized Cells

Single-celled organisms can get along quite well on their own. Even an amoeba, which seems like just a simple cell, can carry out many different tasks as it moves through the environment searching for food and avoiding dangers. More complex organisms, however, consist of many different kinds of cells. Each kind is specialized to do one particular set of tasks very well, but it has lost some other abilities that single-celled organisms have.

Let's take a look at the cells in your body, for example. You have specialized cells in your brain, liver, blood, skin, muscles, and other parts of your body. Each kind of cell has a special job to do. The cells of your body work well together. You can walk and talk and play because the many different kinds of cells cooperate. As long as each kind is doing its share, your body will function normally and stay healthy.

Cell Talk

The many kinds of cells in the body are all busy doing their own thing. But they must be able to work together. So the cells in your body are constantly "talking" to each other. Cells communicate by sending out messages in the form of chemicals. These may be picked up by receptors on the membranes of nearby cells, or they may be carried by the bloodstream to faraway organs.

When a receptor on the outside of a cell picks up a messenger chemical, it passes the message on through the membrane into the cytoplasm. The signal from the receptor may start up a series of reactions inside the cell. They may cause the cell to grow, or stop growing, to speed up the release of energy from food, or to produce proteins to send out to other cells.

Chemical messages can even cause a cell to commit suicide! That is one way the body keeps diseases under control—by commanding infected or damaged cells to let their lysosome enzymes destroy the cell contents. "Programmed cell death" also plays an important role in development. It is a way to get rid of old structures to make way for new ones—for example, in the shaping of fingers, toes, and other body parts.

General Body Cells

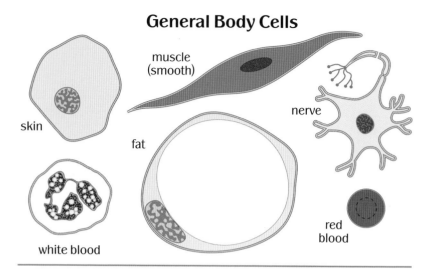

muscle (smooth)

nerve

skin

fat

white blood

red blood

Immune System Cells

macrophage lymphocyte neutrophil dendritic

Body cells are quite varied, but each contains the usual set of organelles. (Mature red blood cells, which lack a nucleus, are an exception.)

How Cells Become Specialized

How do cells know which jobs they are supposed to do? All the cells in a complex organism—whether they are in the brain, heart, or liver—start out as a group of generalized cells in a young embryo (an organism in its early stages of development). All these cells have the same set of chromosomes, containing instructions for the whole organism.

But as the embryo grows and its cells divide, certain genes are turned on in one kind of cell, while different genes are turned on in other kinds of cells. (Most of the genes in a cell are actually "turned off" most of the time.) Genes direct the production of proteins. As each cell makes its own particular kinds of proteins, it becomes different from the other cells in the embryo. With each successive cell division, the various kinds of cells become more and more different.

This process, in which cells become different and specialized, is known as differentiation. Cells differentiate to form the various parts of the body, each with its own function. The specialized cells group together to form body tissues. A grouping of tissues in a specific structure forms an organ, such as a heart or kidney in an animal or a leaf or stamen in a plant.

This plant's leaves are made up of groups of cells that form a specific structure.

Scientists are still learning how differentiation works and what controls turn genes on and off. They hope someday to use "on-off switches" to allow people to repair damaged organs and even to grow new body parts. In Chapter 6, you'll find out more about the exciting progress in this area.

Skin and Lining Cells

Every organ in your body is wrapped in a covering of special cells called epithelium. In fact, your whole body is wrapped in a covering of epithelial cells, called the epidermis. The epidermis is the outer layer of your skin.

The openings into the body and the spaces inside the organs are also lined with epithelial cells. The soft, moist surface inside your nose and mouth, for example, is made of epithelial cells.

These epithelial cells are found on the outer layer of skin.

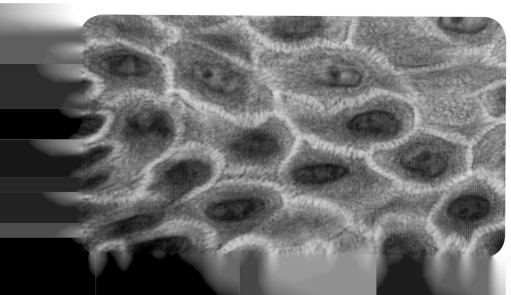

It's a Matter of Color

Everybody has a dark-colored pigment in their skin cells, called melanin. This pigment comes in tiny bundles. It helps to shield us from the sun's harmful rays. When we are out in the sun, the bundles of melanin in the skin get larger, and our skin gets darker. Some people have more melanin in their skin than others. That's why some people have darker skin than others.

Animal skins often contain melanin. Sometimes they have other pigments as well, which give their bodies different colors. Some animals, such as chameleons, flounder, and frogs, can even change their color. They may become darker or lighter, depending on how the tiny bundles of pigment are spread out in the skin cells. Color changes can act as camouflage to help the animals blend in to their surroundings.

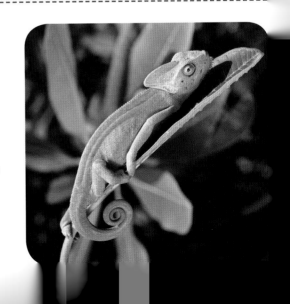

Chameleons can turn many colors to match their surroundings. This chameleon has changed colors to match the leaf.

The epithelium that lines the tiny air sacs in your lungs is so thin that gases can pass freely through it. That is how the oxygen you breathe into your lungs gets into the rest of your body.

Bits of digested food pass through the epithelium lining the intestines and enter your blood. There they are carried to the proper places in your body where they may be used as energy or to help you grow. Without this absorption through the intestinal epithelium, you would starve, even if your stomach was filled with food.

Some very specialized epithelial cells form structures called glands. Their job is to make chemicals for the body. Some glands just pour out their chemicals, to be used in the nearby area. Glands in the skin, for example, secrete oil that helps to keep the skin soft and smooth. Sweat glands in the skin secrete a watery liquid that carries away excess heat from the body. Glands in the eyes produce tears that keep the eyeballs from drying out. Glands in the lining of the stomach and the intestines produce enzymes and other chemicals that help to digest the food you eat.

Some glandular cells produce chemicals that act on the whole body. They secrete these chemicals, called hormones, into the blood, which carries them to the places where they are needed. A "master gland," the pituitary, helps to control and coordinate the secretion of hormones by other glands.

The epithelial cells of many animals produce some structures made of nonliving substances. The hairs, whiskers, and fur of mammals consist mainly of a protein called keratin. A mammal's fur traps air and acts like a blanket to keep its body warm; a bird's feathers do the same job. The skin cells of insects make a tough outer cover containing a substance called chitin. Chitin coats an insect from head to foot and lines the inside of its digestive system as well. The chitin coat is like a suit of armor, which protects the insect and serves as its skeleton. (An insect does not have bones like you do.)

Insects have chitin coats that serve as their skeleton. Here a cicada has molted, or shed, its outer skeleton (below).

Plants have covering cells too. A green leaf or stem is covered with an epidermis layer. These special cells make a waxy substance, which acts as a smooth, waterproof "raincoat" for the leaf.

On the underside of a green leaf, there are special epidermis cells called guard cells. These come in pairs and look like two tiny kidney beans. They are placed side by side so that there is a small hole, called a stomate, in the middle. Thousands

The surface of this tobacco leaf shows several opened and unopened stomates with their surrounding guard cells. The guard cells control how much water vapor and carbon dioxide pass through the stomates.

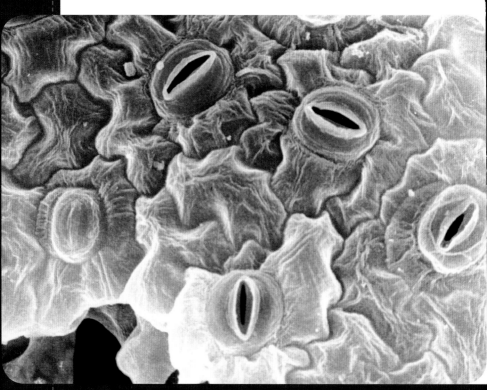

of stomates lie on the bottom of each leaf. The guard cells are like little mouths, opening and closing according to how much sunlight there is and how much moisture is in the air. A plant "breathes" through these openings.

The roots of a plant are covered with a very delicate epidermis. These root cells act rather like the epithelial cells that line our intestines. They take in water and salts from the soil. Plants use the water and salts, along with gases that come in through the guard cells, to make their own food.

Blood Cells

Every second, your heart pumps blood through a network of branching tubes called blood vessels. Blood contains billions of red blood cells. All these red cells are rich in hemoglobin, a protein that gives blood its red color. Hemoglobin carries oxygen from the lungs to the body cells. It also carries carbon dioxide waste from the body cells to the lungs, where it is breathed out of the body.

The red blood cells aren't the only cells that travel in the bloodstream. For every thousand red blood cells there are one or two white blood cells. These cells are jellylike blobs that have no fixed shape, just like the amoebas that live in a pond. Like amoebas, white blood cells can swim or creep along and can change their shape. Some of them can even gobble up smaller living cells, just as amoebas do.

The white blood cells act as a combination of defending army and cleanup squad. They patrol the body and go after foreign invaders, such as bacteria. The job of some white cells is to recognize things that do not belong in the body; others

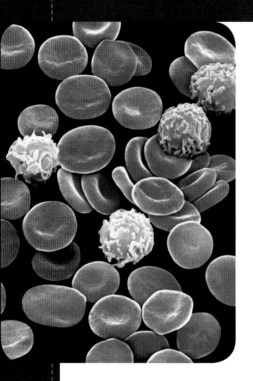

Many disk-shaped red blood cells surround a few spherical white blood cells.

produce weapons, such as proteins called antibodies, that kill or control invaders. Still others roam through the tissues and gobble up germs and bits of debris from damaged body cells.

Cells That Help You Move

Put your hand on your chest. Do you feel a thumping? Of course that's your heart. Your heart is really a muscle, beating away day and night, pushing oxygen-rich blood throughout your body. In addition to your heart, you have muscles in just about every part of your body—your arms, legs, neck, back, and deep inside you. All these muscles are made up of thousands or even millions of muscle cells. These cells work together in bundles.

We could not move at all without muscles. The muscles attached to your bones help you move your arms and legs, to bend over and straighten up. Muscles also provide support. If you look at a skeleton, you'll notice that unless it is carefully tied together and hung from something, it will collapse into a pile of bones. In a living human, it is the muscles pulling on the bones of the skeleton that keep the body standing up.

When you want to move your legs or arms, the muscles in them contract (tighten). All cells can contract a little, but muscle cells are very good at it. When muscles contract, they help you to do work. You lift things with your arm muscles and chew your food with your jaw muscles. Muscles move your eyeballs, and muscles in your stomach churn the food you eat. Many muscles work in pairs. For example, a big muscle on the front of your upper arm (biceps) makes your arm bend up at the elbow. A muscle on the back of your upper arm (triceps) contracts when you straighten out your arm.

This smooth muscle in the intestines is contracting, shown in the wavy lines running through the muscle.

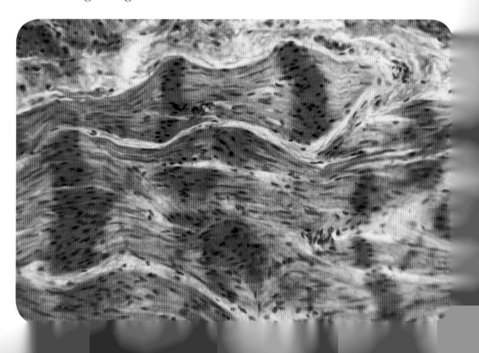

The muscles of other animals are made up of bundles of muscle cells very much like ours. But in some animals the muscles are arranged quite differently. The earthworm, for instance, has two sets of muscles. Longitudinal muscles run along the worm's body, from head to rear; circular muscles form circles around the worm's body. When an earthworm moves through the soil, it contracts each set of muscles in turn. Contracting the circular muscles makes the worm's body long and thin, and it stretches forward. Then

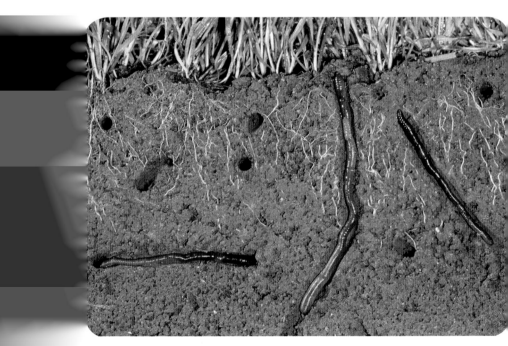

These earthworms use both sets of muscles—longitudinal and circular—to move through the soil.

contractions of its longitudinal muscles make it bulge out in a ring, wedging its front part in place while it draws the rest of its body forward. (We humans also have some circular and longitudinal muscles—in our intestines, where they work to mix and churn the food being digested.)

An insect's muscles are attached to the inside of its tough chitin coat. The muscles can move body parts because

Clams have such strong muscles holding their two shells together that the muscles have to be cut with a knife in order to open them.

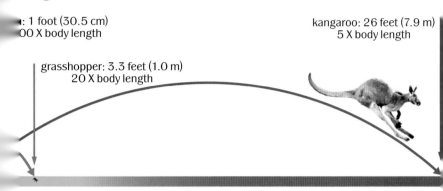

: 1 foot (30.5 cm)
00 X body length

grasshopper: 3.3 feet (1.0 m)
20 X body length

kangaroo: 26 feet (7.9 m)
5 X body length

A flea may not jump far, but compared to its body length, it can outjump a grasshopper and even a kangaroo. All three animals use muscle power to jump.

the chitin "skeleton" is jointed. Muscles move the wings of insects that fly, and muscles in the hind legs of jumping insects power their long jumps. A grasshopper can jump twenty times the length of its body, and a tiny flea can jump two hundred times its own body length! Compare that to a kangaroo, which can jump only five times its length.

Although nearly all animals have muscle cells, plants do not have any at all. Plants move only by growing. Plant cells have specialized growing areas called meristems in the root and shoot tips. Growth in the meristem makes the plant grow taller and extends its root system. Another area, called the cambium, makes the plant grow wider and thicker around the stems. A plant's movement is much slower than the way muscles work.

Messenger Cells

Would you believe that you have miles and miles of "wires" in your body? Like the telephone wires that crisscross through a city, the "wires" in your body carry messages from one place to another. Actually, they are not wires at all, but long thin cells, called nerve cells, or neurons.

Some neurons are very short, only as long as the period at the end of a sentence. But others are longer than your arm. The nerve cells that run down the neck of a giraffe may be more than 10 feet (3 m) long. But even a giraffe's neurons cannot be seen without a microscope. That's because nerve cells are extremely thin—thinner than the hairs on your head or the strands of a spider web.

There is a whole network of nerve cells in the body. The centers of this network

The nerve cells in a giraffe's neck can be 10 feet (3 meters) long but still can't be seen without the help of a microscope.

are the brain and a long cord of nerves that runs down the back, called the spinal cord.

Your brain is filled with billions of nerve cells. They are responsible for your thoughts, memories, and even your mood. They also let you know what's going on in the world around you and help in all your everyday activities.

Like telephone wires, many neurons are covered in layers of insulation, which keep the messages from going astray. This covering is known as the myelin sheath. Unlike telephone wires, nerve cells can carry messages in only one direction.

Some neurons carry messages to the brain and spinal cord from all parts of the body. Many of these carry messages from the sense organs, such as the eyes, ears, or nose. These nerve cells are called sensory neurons.

Other neurons carry messages from the brain and spinal cord to other parts of the body. For example, these messages tell glands to produce chemicals or muscles to contract. Without these messages, you could not move. These kinds of nerve cells are called motor neurons.

When you watch a car whizzing by or a child playing across the street, your eyes send messages through sensory neurons to your brain. Your brain decodes the messages, and you see. Whenever you want to move a foot, a hand, or even a finger, the brain sends messages through motor neurons to the right muscles, and you move.

While we depend on nerve cells to function in life, plants have no nerve cells at all. Yet plants are alive—they move and breathe and grow. The messages in plants are carried by chemicals. They travel much more slowly than the messages carried by our nerves. That is one of the reasons why plants move more slowly than animals.

Cells That Connect

Connective tissue is made up of various kinds of cells that connect, support, or surround other tissues and organs. It gives your body a basic structure and shape. Without connective tissue, your body would be like a blob of jelly. Types of connective tissue include bones, ligaments, and tendons.

Saving It for Later

When you eat, your body breaks down the food to be absorbed into the body. Some of the food chemicals can be used right away. Any excess fat that cannot be used is stored in fat cells. Fat cells are a type of connective tissue that can be found all over the body. Their job is to store fat. It can be used as energy later on when the body needs it. When a fat cell gets filled, it plumps up. The more you eat, the bigger your fat cells get, and the more you weigh. When you lose weight, the stored fat disappears, but the fat cells themselves remain—ready to fill up again.

An important feature of this tissue is that its cells produce a matrix, a layer of nonliving matter that surrounds the cells. The matrix may be liquid or solid, loose or compact, flexible or hard. It forms a kind of framework for bone, blood vessels, or other body structures.

Fibroblasts are among the most common cells in connective tissue. These cells surround major organs, blood vessels, and epithelial tissues. Fibroblasts produce fiberlike proteins that are woven into a kind of mesh. The most important of these proteins, collagen, acts as a glue and support.

Cartilage is a very flexible, yet tough, form of connective tissue. In some animals, such as sharks

Cartilage consists of widely spaced cells surrounded by a thick matrix of collagen fibers.

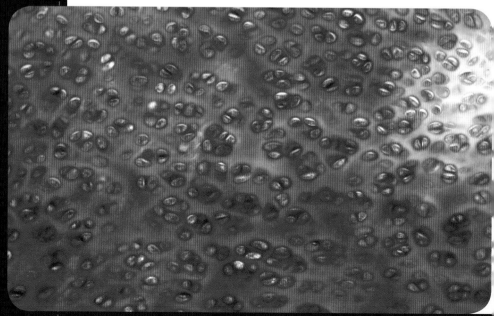

and stingrays, the entire skeleton is made of cartilage. In humans, cartilage is found only at the ends of bones in joints, such as the knee or elbow, and in flexible parts of the body, such as the ear and the tip of the nose.

Bones provide the basic structure of your body. They also act as a support and protection for the body and its organs. Bones are strong and hard, but they are made by the same cells that first lay down a matrix of cartilage. (When you were born, much of your skeleton was made of cartilage.) Special bone-building cells called osteoblasts, which means "bone formers," lay down deposits of calcium and phosphorus on the cartilage matrix. These deposits harden into a sturdy bone. Some of these bone-building cells make new bone cells. That's how your bones grow. If you break a bone, the osteoblasts will make new cells to heal the break. Bone building and reshaping are processes that go on all the time. So to keep your bones strong, it is important to eat foods containing plenty of calcium.

Another kind of bone cell also plays an important part in the growth of bones. These cells are called osteoclasts, which means "bone breakers." Osteoclasts and osteoblasts work together to keep your bones healthy. Osteoclasts eat away small parts of bones. This releases calcium, phosphate, and other minerals into the bloodstream. The osteoblasts fill in the areas of missing bone with layers of collagen. Calcium and other minerals are added to the crisscrossing layers of collagen fibers to create new, hard bone. This process will continue until you are about thirty-five years old. Then it slows down, and the bones start to become thinner and weaker.

Snails have an outer shell made of a hard material that protects their bodies.

Some animals have quite different kinds of skeletons supporting their bodies. We've already learned that insects have chitin skeletons on the outside. The bodies of certain other types of animals, such as clams, snails, and crabs, are encased in shells made of lime or some other hard material. And some small, soft-bodied animals, such as the various worms, have no skeletons at all.

Plants do not have bones. But they do have a sort of skeleton that holds them up. Trees have a very firm structure. The skeleton of a tree is made up of an inner core of xylem tissue (which is actually most of the trunk itself, and a large portion of each branch). The xylem in the outer layer of the trunk carries water and dissolved minerals up through the tree. But the xylem tissue in the core is dead, and its thick-walled cells are pressed tightly together to form solid wood.

The stalk of a daisy and even a blade of grass have skeletons, too. Compared to a tree, the amount of xylem in these plants is very small. They have other types of tissue that help to stiffen them, but their skeletons are mainly made up of water. What happens is that the cells of the plant take in enough water to make them firm and to provide strength.

Ever since Antoni van Leeuwenhoek first observed cells under a microscope back in the seventeenth century, scientists have been trying to get a close look inside cells, hoping to uncover the mysteries of their contents. Modern advances in microscopes and imaging techniques have made it possible to see cells and their inner structures in precise detail. In organs like the brain, which contain many different types of cells, the study of single cells can provide new knowledge and insights into how the organ does its work.

Researchers at a number of universities have been working on techniques that can look deep inside a single cell. They can analyze separate parts of cells and even make videos of the events that occur inside cells at the microscopic level. Their tools range from high-powered microscopes to fluorescent dyes that make particular chemicals light up. With these tools, researchers can see each individual organelle in a single cell and learn about its workings.

Artificial Cloning

In nature, cloning—a process that creates exact copies of genetic material, cells, or entire multicellular living organisms—is a natural, everyday occurrence. We know that single-celled organisms, such as amoebas and paramecia, reproduce by splitting into two. The single cell divides to form two identical daughter cells—each one containing the exact same DNA. These offspring are clones of their parent.

A researcher studies cells under a microscope in Spain.

Many more complex, multicellular plants can reproduce by producing small plants that are genetically identical to the plant from which they grow. For example, the kalanchoe plant produces tiny plantlets in the notches along the edges of its leaves. If a leaf breaks off and falls to the ground, each of the little plantlets can grow into a new plant identical to its mother. Humans and other animals can also reproduce

These triplets are technically clones of one another because they have an identical genetic makeup.

clones: identical twins, triplets, or even sextuplets— each with the same genetic makeup (but not identical to that of either parent).

After years of research and experimenting, scientists have found out how to work with cells and control the cloning process. Early in 1997, the world was stunned by the announcement that Scottish researchers had produced a clone from a cell taken from an adult sheep. How was this accomplished? The first step was to destroy the nucleus of a sheep egg cell. Researchers then removed the nucleus from a body cell of another sheep, the one that was to be cloned. This donor nucleus was injected into the egg cell. The egg cell now had a new nucleus, which was then transplanted into the uterus of an unrelated "surrogate mother" sheep. The egg developed inside her body, producing a lamb with the same genetic makeup as the donor.

Normally, a newborn animal conceived in the usual way develops from a brand-new cell, a fertilized egg. But this lamb, Dolly, started out her life as a set of chromosomes

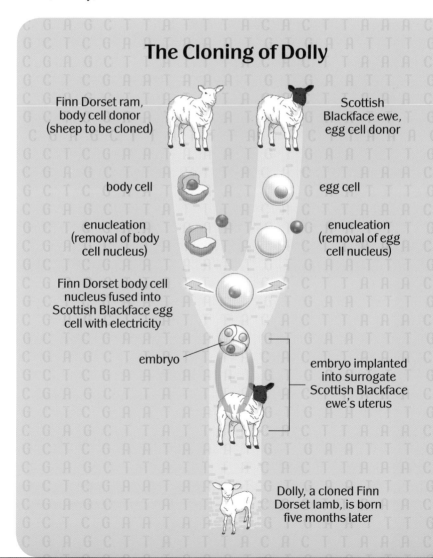

The Cloning of Dolly

Finn Dorset ram, body cell donor (sheep to be cloned)

Scottish Blackface ewe, egg cell donor

body cell

egg cell

enucleation (removal of body cell nucleus)

enucleation (removal of egg cell nucleus)

Finn Dorset body cell nucleus fused into Scottish Blackface egg cell with electricity

embryo

embryo implanted into surrogate Scottish Blackface ewe's uterus

Dolly, a cloned Finn Dorset lamb, is born five months later

Dolly was the first animal to be genetically cloned from adult cells.

containing the hereditary information of a sheep who was already six years old. Some scientists were afraid that Dolly might not grow normally. However, Dolly grew into a healthy young sheep. She mated, and the following spring she gave birth to a healthy lamb of her own.

Researchers all over the world tried to use the new methods to clone other animals. Various groups successfully cloned cows, pigs, and mice. Achievements in cloning research included the first cloned housecat, CC (for CopyCat), born in Texas in 2002, and the first cloned dog, Snuppy, produced by South Korean researchers in 2005. Meanwhile, debates raged in the media as people speculated on the eventual cloning of humans. Would this be morally acceptable? Should work on human cloning be banned?

The original aims of the researchers had nothing to do with cloning humans. They were trying to

Cells

find ways to reproduce exact copies of particular agricultural animals—for example, cows that give an exceptionally large amount of milk—without the uncertainties of breeding. Cloning could also be a method for reproducing animals whose genes had been changed genetically to produce desirable traits.

Cloning could also be used to reproduce animals of species that are close to extinction in the wild. In 2001, researchers in Massachusetts cloned a gaur, a rare type of cattle from India. They inserted the nuclei from skin cells of an adult male gaur into 692 egg cells from ordinary cows. Forty of them developed into embryos, which were placed in the bodies of cow surrogate mothers. Only one of them produced a healthy gaur calf, named Noah. The same research group cloned a banteng (an endangered cattle species from Asia) in 2003. Stockings, the banteng calf, was cloned from a skin cell taken from a banteng that died in 1980. The skin sample had been frozen for more than twenty years before it produced a healthy "offspring." Like Noah, Stockings developed in the body of an ordinary cow mother.

Many scientists have serious doubts about using cloning as an artificial form of reproduction. They point to the many failures in efforts to produce clones. It took 276 tries, for example, to produce Dolly, the first cloned sheep. Researchers at the University of Missouri used 3,000 cloned embryos to try to produce the first cloned piglets. They wound up with only seven cloned piglets.

Success rates have improved as scientists worked out the best techniques for each cloned species. However, some cloned animals, which seemed healthy at birth, soon showed

signs of aging. When Dolly was only three, for
example, researchers noticed that cells in her body
were showing signs of wear more typical of an older
animal. At five-and-a-half, she developed arthritis.
The following year she began to develop a serious
lung disease. These are ailments that normally strike

Real-Life Jurassic Park?

Could scientists *really* re-create dinosaurs, as in the
popular movie *Jurassic Park*? Right now, it is still
just science fiction. But serious researchers have
proposed using cloning to re-create another extinct
species, the woolly mammoth.

At the World Expo 2005, Japanese researchers
showed off a mammoth that had been preserved in
ice in Siberia for more than 18,000 years. Working
with a team of Russian scientists, they hoped
to clone a mammoth using frozen cells or DNA.
However, the DNA of the mammoths found up to
that time was too badly broken down to use.

Then, in 2007, a Siberian reindeer hunter found the
frozen body of a baby mammoth that had died when
it was about six months old—about 37,000 years

sheep twice her age. (Remember, her DNA was taken from a sheep that was already six years old.)

Scientists do not yet agree on whether premature aging is a general problem that will affect most or all cloned animals. Time and more experience in cloning different species may answer this question.

---

ago. "Lyuba" was almost perfectly preserved, with its eyes, trunk, and some fur still intact. Zoo director Aleksei Tikhonov at the Russian Academy of Sciences believes that even Lyuba is not well enough preserved to use its cells for cloning. Freezing, he points out, would have caused its cells to burst. But an international team of researchers has been mapping the DNA from frozen mammoth tissues. (Even though the DNA is broken into pieces, the fragments from different cells overlap. They can be put together like a puzzle to figure out the whole sequence in each chromosome.)

The researchers plan to compare mammoth DNA with that of modern elephants. Then parts of the elephant DNA could be changed to make them more like the mammoth genes. Eventually scientists could make copies of mammoth chromosomes in living elephant cells and use these cells for cloning a mammoth.

Stem Cell Research

Medical researchers have been making progress in promising new research that uses stem cells. These are cells from an early stage of development that have not yet differentiated. When separated, each one has the potential to produce any of the tissues and organs needed for a fully independent individual. For instance, a stem cell can grow into a kidney, heart muscle, or brain tissue. Transplants of stem cells can be used to repair tissues that are damaged by injury or disease. Medical experts hope this kind of cell therapy can help in the treatment of conditions like Parkinson's disease, Alzheimer's disease, and spinal

This scanning electron micrograph gives a 3-D view of human embryonic stem cells. These stem cells have grown and formed into a horizontal strand.

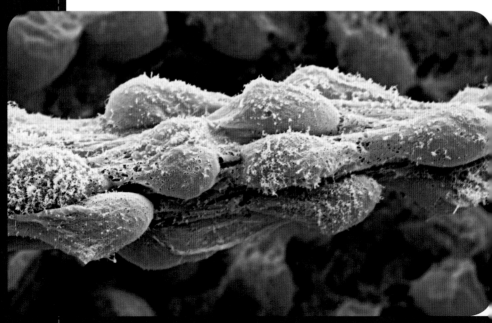

cord injury. Stem cells could also be used to grow replacement organs such as livers, lungs, and hearts.

An important focus of stem cell research is the nervous system. Under normal conditions, if nerve cells in the brain and spinal cord are damaged, they do not grow back. Each body cell is bathed in a fluid that contains a varied mixture of chemicals, from simple salts to proteins and other complex biochemicals. Some of these stimulate growth and others prevent growth. When nerve tissue is damaged, the connections between neurons are broken and they cannot transmit messages. When this happens to motor nerves (those that control muscle movements), paralysis can result—the body part can no longer move. Studies using animals such as rats have shown that when stem cells taken from embryos are transplanted into a site where nerves have been damaged, the cells can grow and restore the broken connections.

How can stem cells develop into functioning nerve tissue? Researchers take the cells from an early-stage embryo, less than a week old, before it has had a chance to form any specific structures. The cells are mixed with growth factors, chemicals that will help them grow and multiply. When the growth factors are removed, the stem cells differentiate into more limited stem cells that form particular kinds of tissues. For example, neural stem cells can form various kinds of nervous-system cells. In 2000, researchers at the National Institute of Neurological Disorders and Stroke (NINDS) transplanted neural stem cells from rat embryos into the brains of rats that had difficulty controlling their movements (similar to the symptoms of Parkinson's disease). After eighty days, the rats showed a 75 percent improvement in their ability to move.

Stem Cell Debate

Research on stem cells has stirred up a lot of controversy. The problem is that the stem cells come from human embryos. Some critics have argued that stem cell research might lead to more abortions. Actually, however, the embryos usually used are the extras left over from in vitro fertilization (joining of an egg and sperm in a culture dish), used to help couples who are unable to conceive children on their own.

Generally, a number of eggs are fertilized to increase the chances of producing a successful pregnancy and birth. The extras are frozen and saved for another try, if necessary. If they are not needed, the embryos are usually thrown away. Thousands of extra embryos are produced in fertility clinics each year. Supporters of stem cell research point out that they are simply using a resource that would be wasted if the embryos were just thrown away.

In 2001 a private company announced that its researchers were creating embryos for stem cell research. These embryos are clones, made by inserting a cell nucleus from a patient into a donor egg whose own nucleus has been destroyed. The patient's body will not reject tissue or organ transplants grown from these stem cells because they have the same genetic information as the patient's cells. Although this kind of work had already been done in mice, the announcement sparked a new debate. Critics said that the researchers were "playing God," creating and destroying human lives.

A key question in the stem cell debate is when human life actually begins. Some people say it starts with the fertilized egg. But others say an embryo is not a true individual until it settles down to develop inside the mother's uterus. Stem cells are obtained from embryos long before this stage.

New studies reported in 2007 and 2008 may eventually settle the stem cell debate by eliminating the use of human embryos. Working first with mice and then with humans, researchers have discovered four key genes that control cell differentiation. The products of these genes bind to the DNA of developing cells and turn other genes on or off. By introducing these four genes into skin cells, the researchers "reprogrammed" the cells, turning them into stem cells. The reprogrammed cells are very similar to embryonic stem cells. They can form any kind of body cells and tissues.

Animal studies of cell therapy for other diseases have also been promising. For example, people with Parkinson's disease have lost many of their brain cells that produce a chemical called dopamine. Researchers in Cambridge, Massachusetts, destroyed the dopamine-producing neurons in the brains of experimental mice, producing Parkinson's like symptoms. In 2008 the researchers reported that treating these mice with dopamine-producing neurons grown from stem cells produced a great improvement of their symptoms. In 2007 the same research team had used cell therapy to cure mice with sickle-cell anemia. Other researchers have been working on using stem cells to repair damaged heart muscle.

Meanwhile, scientists are learning more about how to direct the growth of stem cells into the particular kind of tissue they want. They have also discovered that various tissues of adults also contain a form of stem cells. It had been known for a long time that cells in tissues that continue to divide throughout life—for example, bone marrow and skin—contain stem cells. In fact, bone marrow transplants to form healthy new blood cells in people with leukemia were the first uses of stem cell therapy. In the 1990s and early 2000s, however, scientists discovered that other organs—including the heart and brain—also contain small numbers of stem cells. Although these adult stem cells have begun to differentiate, they still have the potential to develop

This graduate student works with stem cell cultures in a lab at the University of California–Irvine.

into a wide variety of cell types. Under the right conditions, they can even form cells of other tissues. Researchers have obtained liver cells from bone marrow stem cells; neural stem cells produced several kinds of blood cells when they were transplanted into bone marrow.

As scientists learn more about how to manipulate the controls of cell growth, they are developing new ways to treat diseases and disabilities. Instead of transplanting stem cells from cultures, these new treatments would work inside the body itself. Drugs would be used to turn old cells into stem cells, or stimulate adult stem cells to grow into new working nerves or muscles or glands. Although these treatments are still experimental, some of these drugs have already been developed. In fact, researchers discovered in 2003 that Prozac and other antidepressants work mainly by stimulating the growth of new neurons in the brain. Some stem cell biologists believe that in the future we may even be able to use the power of stem cells to help the body replace body parts lost in accidents.

Cell Fusion

Another area with future possibilities is cell fusion. Cells taken from two different species are specially treated in a culture dish and literally join together (fuse), merging their contents. As a result, a hybrid cell is formed, which carries the chromosomes of both "parents." Some very unusual hybrid cells have been produced in the laboratory, such as mouse-hamster, mouse-human, and even plant-animal combinations. When the hybrid cells multiply in a culture dish, they tend to lose some of their chromosomes. In mouse-human cell hybrids, for example, most of the human chromosomes are eventually lost; researchers are not yet sure why this happens. But some chromosomes remain, and the genes they contain produce their characteristic proteins.

Some researchers have suggested using cell fusion to introduce genes into cells of people with genetic diseases. This kind of "fix," for example, might cure people with sickle-cell anemia and cystic fibrosis.

Cell fusion already has a number of other valuable uses. Hybrid cells are helping researchers to map chromosomes—to determine which genes are found on which chromosomes. Since the hybrids lose some chromosomes, the hybrid cells will be unable to make the proteins linked to the lost genes. Analyzing the proteins made by the hybrid cells shows researchers which chromosomes contain the genes for the missing proteins.

By studying hybrid cells, researchers can also find out more about how genes are turned on and off as an organism develops. Studies at the National Cancer Institute, for example, found that when mouse blood cells are fused with human blood cells, the hybrid produces both mouse and human hemoglobins. But if a mouse blood cell is fused with a human skin cell, it forms only mouse hemoglobin. Apparently the genes for human blood chemicals are turned off in skin cells and their hybrids.

A genetic research scientist studies chromosomes with a microscope and computer. Cell fusion and hybrid cells are helping scientists map chromosomes and learn more about genes.

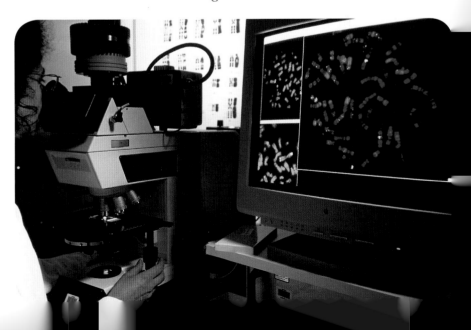

Cell fusion is also used to mass-produce very specific antibodies (germ-fighting proteins). These antibodies are used to test for various biochemicals and to treat many diseases. To make the antibodies, antibody-producing cells are fused (joined) with cancer cells to produce hybrid cells called hybridomas. Antibody-producing cells are rather hard to grow in culture, but cancer cells multiply rapidly in huge numbers. The hybridomas inherit the antibody-making traits of one cell parent and the fast-growing

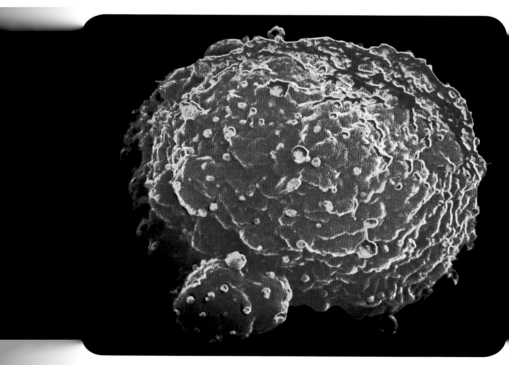

This artificially colored scanning electron micrograph shows a single hybridoma cell.

characteristics of the other (the cancer cell). Therefore, the hybridomas can be grown in cell cultures to produce huge amounts of antibodies, far more than could be obtained from an animal.

Today's exciting cell research is providing new insights into how the body works, what happens when things go wrong, and ways to help us live longer, healthier lives. More research will be needed to turn these discoveries into practical treatments. Cell biologists hope their work will lead to medical miracles— new ways of treating, diagnosing, and preventing diseases and perhaps even ways of reversing the aging process.

Glossary

anaphase: the stage of mitosis in which the centromeres split and the sister chromatids move to opposite poles of the spindle

anther: a male reproductive organ of a plant; produces sperm cells

antibodies: special proteins produced by white blood cells. Some antibodies kill or control germs.

asexual reproduction: a form of reproduction in which a single individual divides to form new individuals exactly like it

ATP (adenosine triphosphate): a chemical compound that can store large amounts of energy and release them readily

binary fission: a form of asexual reproduction by which a cell splits into two daughter cells

bud: the result of budding, an asexual process by which offspring develop as an outgrowth of a parent

cambium: specialized growing area in plants that helps them grow wider and thicker around the stems

capsule: a slimy, protective outer layer found on some bacteria

cartilage: the tough, stretchy tissue at the ends of bones in adults. Cartilage makes up most of the skeleton in young children.

cell: the basic unit of life

cell division: the process by which one cell divides into two

cell plate: the plant cell wall material deposited midway between the daughter cells during cytokinesis

cell theory: the belief that all living things are made up of cells and that cells are the basic unit of life

cellulose: a tough material that is a major part of most plant cell walls

cell wall: a tough, rigid outer covering surrounding a cell. In plants, the cell wall contains cellulose. In bacteria, however, the cell wall does not contain cellulose.

centriole: a tiny organelle, located in the cytoplasm near the nucleus, that divides perpendicularly during mitosis and meiosis in animal cells

centromere: a structure that joins two identical chromatids

chiasmata: points at which maternal and paternal chromosomes overlap

chitin: a substance that makes up most of the tough outer covering of insects, crustaceans, and arachnids

chlorophyll: the green pigment in plant cells that gathers light energy

chloroplasts: structures in plant cells in which photosynthesis occurs

chromatid: one of a pair of duplicated chromosomes

chromatin: DNA-protein fibers that, during prophase, condense to form the visible chromosomes

chromoplast: a plastid containing pigment

chromosomes: threadlike structures in a cell's nucleus that carry DNA

cloning: a process that produces a cell, cell product, or organism that contains genetic material identical to the original

collagen: a tough protein fiber found in connective tissue

connective tissue: tissues that protect, support, and hold together the internal organs and other structures of animals. These tissues include bone, cartilage, tendons, and other tissues.

crossing over: the process by which maternal and paternal chromosomes exchange genetic material, creating new combinations of genes

cytokinesis: the division of the cell cytoplasm

cytoplasm: the substance between the cell membrane and the nucleus (or the nuclear body in prokaryotes)

differentiation: a process by which cells become different and specialized

diploid: a type of cell that has two of each kind of chromosome

DNA (deoxyribonucleic acid): the chemical basis of hereditary traits

embryo sac: a large cell in a plant seed, within which the embryo develops

endoplasmic reticulum (ER): a network of tubular membranes that extends out from the nuclear membrane

endosperm: a portion of a plant seed that contains stored food

epidermis: the outer layer of living skin cells

epithelium: tissue covering body surfaces or lining the internal surfaces of body openings, cavities, and hollow organs

eukaryote: an organism whose cell or cells contain a nucleus surrounded by a membrane

fertilization: the process by which egg and sperm nuclei come together to form a zygote

fibroblasts: fiber-forming cells that make the framework for skin and connective tissues

flagella (*singular* **flagellum):** long, hairlike structures that extend from the organism to help it move

gamete: a haploid reproductive cell (either a sperm or an egg)

genes: chemical units that determine hereditary traits passed on from one generation of cells or organisms to the next

germ cell: a sex cell before it has fully matured

glands: structures that make chemicals for the body

Golgi complex: also known as Golgi apparatus or Golgi bodies; a cell organelle that consists of membrane bags, involved in sorting and storing products needed by the cell

guard cells: epidermis cells on the underside of a plant leaf

haploid: a type of cell that has only one of each kind of chromosome

hemoglobin: a red-colored protein that helps the red blood cells carry oxygen to cells all over the body

homologous chromosomes: chromosomes that bear genes for the same characteristics

hormones: chemicals secreted into the bloodstream, which control and regulate the body's activities

hybrid: a cell that forms as a result of joining cells from two different species

hybridoma: a hybrid cell that combines the characteristics of an antibody-forming cell and those of cancer cells

hydrophilic: "water-loving," i.e., mixing readily with water

hydrophobic: "water-fearing," i.e., mixing readily with fats and oils but not with water

interphase: a preliminary stage of cell division in which the cell grows and prepares for the actual division by first making a copy of its DNA

leucoplast: a colorless plastid that stores food such as starch

lysosome: a small, round organelle that functions in the digestion of materials within the cell

matrix: a layer of nonliving matter that surrounds the cells and helps to form a kind of framework

meiosis: the division process that produces cells with one-half the number of chromosomes in each daughter cell

melanin: dark pigment in the skin

meristem: specialized growing area in plants that helps them grow taller and extend their root system; located in the root and shoot tips

metaphase: the stage of mitosis or meiosis in which the chromatids line up along the equatorial plane in the middle of the cell

metaphase plate: an imaginary line within a dividing cell in which the duplicated chromosomes become aligned during metaphase

mitochondrion (*plural* **mitochondria):** an organelle in the cell cytoplasm that has its own DNA and produces energy to power the cell's activities

mitosis: the process of nuclear division producing daughter cells with exactly the same number of chromosomes as in the mother cell

motor neurons: nerve cells that carry messages from the brain to various parts of the body to make muscles move

myelin sheath: a covering that wraps around neurons to provide a continuous flow of chemical messages

neuron: nerve cell

nuclear membrane: a two-layered covering that surrounds the nucleus of a living cell; also called nuclear envelope

nucleoid: the nuclear area in prokaryotes that contains the cell's DNA

nucleolus (*plural* nucleoli): a small, rounded body within the nucleus of a cell, functioning in ribosome manufacture

nucleus: the control center of the cell, which contains its hereditary instructions and is surrounded by a membrane separating the nucleus from the rest of the cell's contents

organ: a grouping of tissues in a specific structure, such as a heart or kidney

organelle: a specialized structure within the cell

osteoblasts: bone-building cells that make new bone tissue

osteoclasts: bone cells that eat away old bone tissue

ovary: the female reproductive organ in animals, which produces eggs. In flowering plants, this structure produces seeds.

ovum (*plural* ova): a female sex cell, also called an egg

photosynthesis: the process by which food (sugars) is produced from carbon dioxide and water, using energy from sunlight

pituitary gland: a sort of "master gland" that helps to control and coordinate the secretion of hormones by other glands

plasma membrane: also called cell membrane; a thin, flexible covering surrounding a cell

plasmid: a strand or loop of DNA that exists independently of the chromosome in bacteria or yeasts

plastid: an organelle in cells of plants and algae, which contains chlorophyll or stored food

prokaryote: a single-celled organism lacking a nucleus surrounded by a membrane

prophase: the first stage of mitosis, in which the chromosomes come together to form two thick rod-shaped chromatids. Prophase I and prophase II are stages in meiosis.

receptor: a docking site on a membrane, into which only a particular kind of chemical fits. The chemical binds to the receptor and either passes through the membrane or triggers a series of reactions inside the cell or organelle.

regeneration: regrowth of body parts that have been lost or injured

ribosome: tiny spherical structure that is involved in manufacturing proteins

RNA (ribonucleic acid): a chemical that carries hereditary information and is involved in manufacturing proteins

sensory neurons: nerve cells that carry messages from the sense organs, such as the eyes, nose, or ears, to the brain and spinal cord

sexual reproduction: a form of reproduction in which a sperm from a male organism joins with an ovum from a female to produce a new individual. This individual has characteristics of both parents.

sperm: a male sex cell

spinal cord: a long cord of nerves that runs down the back and is responsible for reflex actions

spindle: a football-shaped structure that forms when the centrioles move apart, pulling out a network of fibers attached to the chromatids

spore: an asexual reproductive body of a fungus or nonflowering plant. The term also refers to a tough, inactive form in which a bacterium can survive under extreme conditions.

stem cells: primitive cells that have the potential to develop into any cells or tissues in the body

stomate: an opening on the underside of a leaf through which a plant takes in and sends out gases

surrogate mother: a female who carries a developing embryo to birth in place of its genetic mother

synapse: a fluid-filled gap where nerve impulses are transmitted from one neuron to another

telophase: the final stage of mitosis or meiosis, in which the chromatids have reached opposite poles, the spindle disappears, the nuclear membrane re-forms, and the chromosomes expand into thin strands of the chromatin

tetrad: a structure that includes four chromatids

tissue: an organized group of cells with a similar structure and a common function

triploid cell: a cell that has three sets of chromosomes

vacuole: a baglike cell structure used for the temporary storage of materials or in the elimination of excess water and waste products from the cell

white blood cells: jellylike blood cells that can move through tissues and are an important part of the body's defenses

xylem: a tissue in plants that provides support and carries water and dissolved minerals up through the plant

zygote: a new cell formed by the joining of an egg and sperm

Bibliography

Aldhouse, Peter. "How Biological 'Alchemy' Can Change a Cell's Destiny." *New Scientist*, June 18, 2008. http://www.newscientist.com/article/ns?id=mg19826613.800 (September 22, 2008).

———. "How Stem-Cell Advances Will Transform Medicine." *New Scientist*, April 30, 2008, 40-43. http://www.newscientist.com/article/mg19826541.100 (September 19, 2008).

Associated Press. "Baby Mammoth Carcass Arrives in Japan for Study." *LJWorld*, December 30, 2007. http://www2.ljworld.com/news/2007/dec/30/baby_mammoth_carcass_arrives_japan_study/ (September 23, 2008).

BBC News. "Mammoth Comes in from the Cold." *BBC News*, October 21, 1999. http://news.bbc.co.uk/2/hi/science/nature/481571.stm (September 23, 2008).

BBC News. "Scientists 'to Clone Mammoth'." *BBC News/Asia-Pacific*, July 18, 2003. http://news.bbc.co.uk/2/hi/asia-pacific/3075381.stm (September 23, 2008).

Dollemore, Doug, and Marjorie Roberts. "Scientists Find that Heart Muscle Cells Regenerate After a Heart Attack." *National Institutes of Health*, June 6, 2001. http://www.nhlbi.nih.gov/new/press/01-06-06.htm (September 23, 2008).

Dove, Alan. "Stem Cells' Self-Renewing Controversy." *Drug Discovery and Development*, February 2008, 24–27.

Emory University Health Sciences Center. "Growth Factor Stimulation Leads to Increase in New Neurons in the Brain." *Biopsychiatry*, August 31, 2001. http://biopsychiatry.com/newbraincell/bdnf.html (September 23, 2008).

Goodsell, David S. *The Machinery of Life*. New York: Copernicus Books, 1998.

Harvard University. "Discovery Could Help Reprogram Adult Cells to Embryonic Stem Cell-like State." *Science Daily*, February 15, 2008. http://www.sciencedaily.com/releases/2008/02/080215130617.htm (September 23, 2008).

Landa, Norbert, and Patrick A. Baeuerle. *The Cell Works.* Hauppauge, NY: Barron's, 1998.

Langreth, Robert, and Matthew Herper. "Stem Cells Get Real." *Forbes*, May 28, 2008. http://www.forbes.com/ healthcare/2008/05/28/stem-cells-biz-healthcare-cx _mh_0528medtech_lander.html (September 23, 2008).

Liveleak. "Scientists Hope DNA Could Clone Baby Mammoth." *Truveo*, March 2008. http://www.truveo .com/scientists-hope-DNA-could-Clone-Baby-Mammoth/ id/527179394 (September 23, 2008).

Llamas Ruiz, Andrés. *The Life of a Cell.* New York: Sterling Publishing Co., 1997.

Milius, Susan. "Cloned Gaur Born Healthy, Then Dies." *Science News*, February 10, 2001. http://www.sciencenews.org/ view/generic/id/1320/title/Cloned_gaur_born_healthy, _then_dies (September 23, 2008).

Rensberger, Boyce. *Instant Biology: From Single Cells to Human Beings, and Beyond.* New York: Fawcett Columbine, 1996.

———. *Life Itself: Exploring the Realm of the Living Cell.* New York: Oxford University Press, 1996.

Roberts, Lynda. "Scientists to Attempt Cloning of Fossilized Baby Mammoth." *Horizons*, April 14, 2008. http:// media.www.eraunews.com/media/storage/paper917/ news/2008/04/14/News/Scientists.To.Attempt.Cloning .Of.Fossilized.Baby.Woolly.Mammoth-3320512.shtml (September 23, 2008).

Rutgers. The State University of New Jersey. "Brain's Recuperative Powers May Be Greater Than Previously Thought." *Nootropics*, March 16, 2001. http://nootropics .com/regenerate/index.html (September 23, 2008).

Silverstein, Alvin, Virginia Silverstein, and Robert Silverstein. *Monerans & Protists.* Brookfield, CT: Twenty-First Century Books, 1996.

University of California–Los Angeles. "Human Skin Cells Reprogrammed Into Embryonic Stem Cells." *Science Daily*, February 12, 2008. http://www.sciencedaily.com/releases/2008/02/080211172631.htm (September 23, 2008).

University of California–Los Angeles. "Researchers Reprogram Normal Tissue Cells Into Embryonic Stem Cells." *Science Daily*, June 7, 2007. http://www.sciencedaily.com/releases/2007/06/070606235430.htm (September 23, 2008).

University Medical Center Utrecht. "Heart Derived Stem Cells Develop Into Heart Muscle." *Science Daily*, April 23, 2008. http://www .sciencedaily.com/releases/2008/04/080423101822.htm (September 23, 2008).

University of Wisconsin–Madison. "Reprogramming the Debate: Stem-cell Finding Alters Ethical Controversy." *Science Daily*, November 22, 2007. http://www.sciencedaily.com/releases/2007/11/071121115002 .htm (September 23, 2008).

Williams, Nigel. "Death of Dolly Marks Cloning Milestone." *Current Biology*, March 18, 2003, R209–R210.

Young, John K. *Cells: Amazing Forms and Functions*. New York: Franklin Watts, 1990.

For Further Information

Books:

Engdahl, Sylvia Louise, ed. *Cloning*. Farmington Hills, MI: Greenhaven Press, 2006.

Fridell, Ron. *Decoding Life: Unraveling the Mysteries of the Genome*. Minneapolis: Twenty-First Century Books, 2005.

———. *Genetic Engineering*. Minneapolis: Lerner Publications, 2006.

Johnson, Rebecca L. *Genetics*. Minneapolis: Twenty-First Century Books, 2006.

Kafka, Tiny. *Cloning*. Farmington Hills, MI: Lucent Books, 2007.

Stewart, Melissa. *Cell Biology*. Minneapolis: Twenty-First Century Books, 2008.

Websites:

Bacterial Cells: The Inside Story
http://www.eurekascience.com/ICanDoThat/bacteria_cells.htm
This site includes links on plant and animal cells, as well as other information on biological processes.

BrainPop – Animated Educational Site for Kids
http://www.brainpop.com/search/?keyword=cells
Tim and Moby introduce you to cells, your basic building blocks. The site also includes movies about stem cells, passive transport, cell structures, cell specialization, and mitosis.

CELLS alive!
http://www.cellsalive.com/toc.htm
This site offers kid-friendly articles on topics including cell division, plant and animal cells, and bacteria. The site also features vivid pictures, movies, and links.

Cells: An Animal Cell

http://www.biology4kids.com/files/cell_main.html
This site offers an overview of the cell and an in-depth look at its parts, including the membrane and various organelles.

How Cells Work

http://www.howstuffworks.com/cell.htm
Marshall Brain presents a comprehensive view of the cell, including structure, enzymes, DNA, reproduction, and biotechnology.

The Human Heart: Blood

http://sln.fi.edu/biosci/blood/blood.html
This Franklin Institute Online site provides basic information about the blood, including red blood cells, white blood cells, and other important aspects of blood.

Stem Cells

http://www.pbs.org/wgbh/nova/sciencenow/3209/04.html
Watch a 15-minute *NOVA* feature on stem cells, vote in a poll on whether we should allow cloning for stem cell research, and read about the cloning process, stem cell politics, and the latest stem cell news. In "Ask the Expert," Harvard researcher Leonard Zon answers questions about stem cell science.

Stem Cells: A Look Inside

http://library.thinkquest.org/04oct/00053/cl_kids.html
This site presents information about stem cells, including laws, ethics, and activities.

Stem Cells in the Spotlight

http://learn.genetics.utah.edu/units/stemcells/
This site offers a thorough treatment of stem cells, with colorful illustrations and animations. Topics include "What is a stem cell?"; different types; health conditions stem cells could be used to treat; a step-by-step examination of developing a stem cell therapy for Parkinson's disease; stem cell therapies in use today and future prospects; how stem cells are created for research; and ethical, legal, and social issues.

Index

Photo Acknowledgments

The images in this book are used with the permission of: © Digital Vision/ Getty Images, p. 5 (top); © Science VU/Visuals Unlimited, Inc., p. 5 (bottom); © Photodisc/Getty Images, pp. 6, 26; The Granger Collection, New York, p. 7; Courtesy of the National Library of Medicine, p. 8; © Time Life Pictures/Mansell/ Getty Images, p. 9; © age fotostock/SuperStock, p. 11; © Dr. Dennis Kunkel/ Visuals Unlimited, Inc., pp. 13, 37, 41; © Wim van Egmond/Visuals Unlimited, Inc., p. 25; © Dr. David M. Phillips/Visuals Unlimited, Inc., pp. 28, 45, 66, 74; © Ralph Hutchings/Visuals Unlimited, Inc., p. 29; © Dr. Fred Hossler/Visuals Unlimited, Inc., p. 35; © Joseph T. Collins/Photo Researchers, Inc., p. 38; © Dwight Kuhn, pp. 42, 53; © iStockphoto.com/Frank Boonstra, p. 46; © Marta Johnson, p. 59; © Dr. John D. Cunningham/Visuals Unlimited, Inc., pp. 60, 67; © Angelo Cavalli/Iconica/Getty Images, p. 61; © George Grall/National Geographic/Getty Images, p. 63; © Dr. Gerald Van Dyke/Visuals Unlimited, Inc., p. 64; © Jacana/Photo Researchers, Inc., p. 68; © Dorling Kindersley/Getty Images, p. 69; © Leonard Lee Rue/Visuals Unlimited, Inc., p. 71; © iStockphoto.com/Sergiy Goruppa, p. 76; © Javier Soriano/AFP/Getty Images, p. 79; © Kate Kunath/Photonica/Getty Images, p. 80; © Getty Images, p. 82; © Professor Miodrag Stojkovic/Photo Researchers, Inc., p. 86; © Sandy Huffaker/ Getty Images, p. 91; © Emakoff/Photo Researchers, Inc., p. 93; © CNRI/Photo Researchers, Inc., p. 94. All illustrations by © Laura Westlund/Independent Picture Service, except p. 81 © Bill Hauser/Independent Picture Service.

Cover: © MedicalRF.com/Getty Images.

About the Authors

Dr. Alvin Silverstein is a former professor of biology and director of the Physician Assistant Program at the College of Staten Island of the City University of New York. Virginia B. Silverstein is a translator of Russian scientific literature.

The Silversteins' collaboration began with a biochemical research project at the University of Pennsylvania. Since then they have produced six children and more than two hundred published books that have received high acclaim for their clear, timely, and authoritative coverage of science and health topics.

Laura Silverstein Nunn, a graduate of Kean College, began helping with the research for her parents' books while she was in high school. Since joining the writing team, she has coauthored more than eighty books.